D0927636

# JAPANESE-ENGLISH
# ENGLISH-JAPANESE

## DICTIONARY AND PHRASEBOOK

# JAPANESE-ENGLISH
# ENGLISH-JAPANESE

## DICTIONARY AND PHRASEBOOK

EVGENY STEINER

HIPPOCRENE BOOKS, INC.
*New York*

Copyright© 2000 Evgeny Steiner
*Second printing, 2003.*

All rights reserved.

ISBN 0-7818-0814-6

For information, contact:
HIPPOCRENE BOOKS, INC.
171 Madison Avenue
New York, NY 10016

Cataloging in Publication data available from the
Library of Congress.

Printed in the United States of America.

# CONTENTS

# INTRODUCTION

This book was designed to help visitors to Japan communicate with local people in typical situations. Each chapter consists of sentences arranged by situation and is complemented by a comprehensive list of related words. The reader can easily use these words in the common phrases and sentences given in the same chapter.

Some parts of this book are set in italics to indicate the way of speaking of the young generation. Young people's language in contemporary Japan differs very much from normative polite language. For example, the sentence "I go"—"Watakushi-wa yukimasu"—is "Boku iku" in young people's language (note "boku" is the first person masculine pronoun). This phrasebook contains many of these expressions and slang words.

In addition, please note that some of the phrases included in the phrasebook can have several grammatical variations while keeping the same meaning. These are indicated here with the use of the backslash. For example, the phrase "How can I get to the Tokyo Tower?", found on page 143, is presented as "Tōkyō tawā-e iku-ni wa /donna norimono-ga arimasu ka/dō ittara ii desu ka?" The question may therefore be translated as either "Tōkyō tawā-e iku-ni wa donna norimono-ga arimasu ka?" or "Tōkyō tawā-e iku-ni wa dō ittara ii desu ka?".

In the Food & Drink section, some expressions are included that might be useful for travelers with certain dietary restrictions, such as keeping kosher or vegetarianism.

# ABBREVIATIONS

| | |
|---|---|
| ad. | adverb |
| adj. | adjective |
| f. | feminine |
| lit. | literally |
| m. | masculine |
| n. | noun |
| nt. | neuter |
| pl. | plural |
| sg. | singular |
| v. | verb |
| v.int. | verb intransitive |
| v.t. | verb transitive |

# A VERY BASIC GRAMMAR AND THE JAPANESE WRITING SYSTEM

## Different Social Forms of Speech

The Japanese employ an extensive system of politeness and honorific markers. The speaker must always keep in mind his/her social relation to the person addressed, and the person he/she is talking about. These markers appear on verbs, adjectives, and even nouns. For example, the informal form of the verb "to go"—*iku*—is used when speaking with someone close to the speaker, but if the person addressed is a stranger or is older than the speaker, the politeness marker *-masu* appears: *iki-masu*. If the person being talked about is socially superior to the speaker, the honorific form of the verb "to go"—*irassharu*—may be used, even if this person is not present. If the person addressed does not have a close relationship with the speaker, or is older, the politeness marker appears on the honorific form: *irasshai-masu*. This form simultaneously allows the speaker to be polite to the person addressed and show respect for the person being talked about. The prefix *o-* (sometimes *go-*) may be used with nouns and adjectives to show politeness or respect to the person addressed or spoken of, as in *o-tsukue* (desk) and o-*suki* (like).

The use of pronouns varies according to social context and often according to gender. The first person pronoun *boku* is used by males in relatively informal situations, while *watashi* is used by females in informal situations and by both males and females in formal situations. There are a large number of ways to express "you", according to social context and gender, including the name of the person addressed. Apart from pronouns in informal speech, the final particles can also vary according to gender.

The use of politeness, honorific markers, and the various pronouns reflect the prominent role that in-group/out-of-group factors play in Japanese. If the person addressed is part of the speaker's "group" in personal relationship or age, the speaker uses the polite style of speech. The terms for family members also reflect this. As a general term for the word "mother" *okā-san* can be used, but it can also mean "my own mother." Thus when calling your own mother, you would say *okā-san*. When talking about your own mother, you would use *haha*, as in **watashi no *haha* wa toshiyori desu** ("my mother is old"). The same distinction is made for the terms for father, sister, brother, etc.

## PRONOUNS

### Personal Pronouns

I **watakushi, watashi; boku** (familiar, in men's speech)
you (singular) **anata**
he/she/it **kare; anohito** (unisex term, meaning "that person")
she **kanojo**

we **watakushitachi; watashitachi; wareware**
you (plural) **anatagata**
they **karera; sorera** (not for human beings)

**Demonstrative Pronouns**

this (closer to speaker) **kore**
this (closer to another person) **sore**
that (distant from both parties) **are**

**Demonstrative Adjectives**

this **kono, sono**
that **ano**

## NOUNS

Nouns have no distinctions for gender and, apart from a limited group of words designating people, no distinction for number (singular and plural). The suffix for the rare plural form is *-tachi*, for example: **watakushi**—I; **watakushitachi**—we.

Markers (particles) following the noun indicate whether a noun is the subject or the object of a sentence.

## PARTICLES

Particles are numerous and very important in Japanese. They play the role of case markers. There are some remnants of a case-marking system in English as well: the pronouns in English change depending on whether it is a subject (he/she/they) or an object (him/her/them). Because of the case markers, the words in Japanese sentences can be placed in different orders and still retain the same meaning.

Particles always follow the words they mark.

**Subject Marker**

The subject is usually marked by *-wa*. It is advisable to say **watakushi-wa...**—I...—and make a pause while you are still considering how to continue. But with the tendency to omit personal pronouns and all other subject nouns which are clear from the context, *-wa* is used less and less in oral speech. Often the appearance of *-wa* indicates a change in subject and thus the introduction of new information, for example:

**Boku-wa konsāto-ni iku.** I'm going to a concert.
**Konsāto-ni iku. Anata-WA?** (I'm) going to a concert. (Are) YOU (going)?

The subject is sometimes emphasized by the particle *-ga*. In many cases it conveys the same meaning as *-wa*. Basically, it is needed in situations where you are not expressing a change in subject, but where you want to emphasize the subject even though it is obvious. Usually, this is done to add emphasis or to avoid ambiguity:

**Chizuko-wa, ashita konsāto-ni iku?** Is (your friend) Chizuko going to the concert tomorrow?

**Iie, ikimasen.** No, (she) doesn't go.
**Nande?** Why not?
**Sore-GA wakaranai-no.** I don't know this.

Here **sore**—this—is emphasized by the particle **-ga**.

The particle **-ga** can also be used as a conjunction:

**Shitsurei desu-GA, anata-wa Suzuki-san desu
ka?** Excuse me, (BUT) are you Mr. Suzuki?

NOTE: **-san** is a polite and unisex form of address,
for example, Mr. Suzuki could also be Mrs. or Miss.

**Possessive Marker**

The possessive case is marked by **-no**. This is the
most common and the simplest particle, for example:

**Watakushi-NO hon.** MY book.
**Watakushi-NO tomodachi-NO nihongo-NO
hon.** MY friend's Japanese book.

**Time Markers**

Time is usually followed by **-ni**. It is used for a specific time or specific spans of time, for example:

**rokugatsu NI** IN June
**jūnigatsu itsuka NI** ON the fifth of December

A word like **ashita**—tomorrow—or **kinō**—yesterday—do not require **-ni**, for example **Ashita iku.**
I'm going tomorrow.

## Place and Tool Marker

The general place of an action or the use of an instrument is followed by *de*, for example:

**O-uchi DE shokuji o suru.** I eat AT home.
**O-hasi DE tabemasu.** I eat WITH chopsticks.
**Kuruma DE iku.** I go BY car.

## Location Marker

The particle *ni* is used to indicate a location, for example:

**Chizuko** (only Chizuku is a family member; if not, the correct form is **Chizuku-san**) **-wa ima o-uchi-NI imasu.** Chizuko is AT home right now.

## Origin/Departure Point Marker

The origin or departure point is marked by *kara*, for example:

**Watakushi-wa Amerika-KARA kimashita.** I came FROM America.
**Shigoto-KARA sugu kaerimasu.** (He) will return FROM his job soon.

## Direct Object Marker

The direct object is followed by *wo*:

**hon-WO yomu** to read a book
**natsu-WO okuru** to spend (the) summer

### Indirect Object Marker

The indirect object is followed by *ni*:

**Chizuko-wa hon-wo yYūjin-NI agemashita.**
  Chizuko gave a book TO Eugene.

"Hon" is the direct object, and "Yujin" is the indirect object in this sentence.

### Destination Marker

The destination is followed by *e*:

**Nihon-E ikitai.** (I) want to go TO Japan.
**Eigakan-E ikimashita.** (I) went TO a movie
  theater.

### Final Point Marker

The final point in time or space is marked by ***made***:

**Gogatsu no mikka-MADE isogashii.** (I'm/I'll
  be) busy UNTIL May third.
**Nyū-Yōku-MADE hikōki-de itte, soko-kara
  kuruma-de ikimashita.** (I) traveled TO New
  York by plane and from there I took a car.
**asa-kara ban-MADE** from morning TO night

### The Particle *mo*

The particle ***mo*** means "too, also" or "both … and …"
(with a positive verb) or "neither … nor …" (with a
negative verb), for example:

**Ashita konsāto-ni iku?** (Are you) going to the
concert tomorrow?

**Un, iku yo, kimi MO?** Yeah, I'm going, you
TOO?

**Boku MO iku.** I'm going TOO.

**Anata-ni MO sore-wo agemasu.** AND to you
ALSO (I'll) give this.

Sometimes *mo* can be used as the conjunction "and":

**Watakushi-wa eigo MO furansugo MO
dekimasu.** I know English AND French.

## ADJECTIVES

There are three types of adjectives in Japanese:
predicative, half-predicative and non-predicative.

### 1. Predicative Adjectives

Predicative adjectives always end with *-i* and have
roots with the vowels a, i, u, or o, for example:

**aka-i** red
**shiro-i** white
**suzushi-i** cool

They can serve as predicates without any verbs or
with a particle *-desu* (in polite style):

**Kono empitsu-wa akai.** This pencil is red.

In negative sentences the root is supplemented by suffix **-ku** + ***arimasen*** (in polite style) or **nai** (in colloquial).

**Kono empitsu-wa akaku naidesu (nai).** This pencil is not red.

## 2. Half-predicative Adjectives

Half-predicative adjectives end with **-ka**, for example **shizuka**—quiet (not loud)—or **-teki**, for example **sei-jiteki**—political—or they are adjectives of Chinese origin, such as **kirei**—beautiful—or **juyo**—important. This type of adjective can function as a predicate only with the verbal form **-desu**:

**Kono heya-wa shizuka desu.** This room is quiet.

Half-predicative adjectives with the suffix **-na** can serve as modifiers to nouns:

**Kore-wa shizukana heya desu.** This is a quiet room.

The suffix **-ni** provides the adverbial meaning:

**Shizukani shinasai!** Be quiet!

## 3. Non-predicative Adjectives

Some adjectives cannot be used as predicates at all. There are only a few, for example:

**aru** a certain (person, object, animal, place)
**iwayuru** so-called

## ADVERBS

Adverbs are formed from predicative adjectives by adding the suffix **-ku** to the root:

**suzushi-ku** cool
**haya-ku** early; quickly
**yasashi-ku** tenderly, softly

## VERBS

As the core element (or keystone) of a sentence, the verb always stands at the end. The verb does not indicate any number or gender. The same form of the verb is used with singular and plural subjects, and no gender distinction is made. The verb also does not take any particles, but it needs to be inflected.

In Japanese, ideas that in other languages are often expressed in separate phrases and sentences frequently take the shape of a single word, albeit a complex one. This is the agglutinative nature of the language. For example, the English sentence "Chizuko was intending (was about) to go and buy a new dictionary for Yujin" contains the separate verbs "was intending (was about)", "to go", and "to buy". In the Japanese sentence, these verbs together form one complex word: **katte-ko-yō-to-shita** (buy—go—was intending—[was about]—past). The verb inflects for tense, negation, aspect, and mood.

There are two main forms of inflections which depend on whether the suffix is **-u** or **-ru**. The first inflection consists of u-verbs, the second one of ru-verbs.

**The First Inflection: U-Verbs**

U-verbs end in a, o, u, k, g, b, m, n, s, t, for example:

**kaku** to write
**oyogu** to swim
**hanasu** to talk
**omou** to think

Typically the *-u* suffix is dropped and a huge variety of suffixes and particles can be added to convey tense, aspect or mood.

There are five main forms of the verb, ending with -a, -i, -u, -e, -o:

kaka (a-form): negative.
With the particle *-nai* it serves to express negation:
**kakanai** do not write

kaki (i-form): substantive, meaning "writing."
It is used with *-masu* in polite speech:
**kakimasu** (I) write

kaku (u-form): neutral or infinitive form "to write."

kake (e-form): indicates demand or an order.
**Hanase!** Speak!
When supplemented with **-ru**, it expresses the ability to do something: **hanaseru** to be able to speak.

<u>kako (o-form)</u>: indicates an invitation: **hanaso** let's speak.

*Other examples:*

**kiku** -> **kiki** listen
**oyogu** -> **oyogi** swim
**yobu** -> **yobi** call
**nomu** -> **nomi** drink
**shinu** -> **shini** die
**tsukuru** -> **tsukuri** make
**matsu** -> **machi** wait
**harau** -> **harai** pay

## Usage of Various Inflected Forms

<u>Replace *-u* with *-ite*</u> for:
a) simple commands
b) doing two things at the same time
(verbs are listed according to phonetic changes)

**hanasu** -> **hanashite** talk

**kiku** -> **kiite** listen (replace entire *-ku*)
**oyogu** -> **oyoide** swim (replace entire *-gu*, be sure to use *-ide*)

**yobu** -> **yonde** call (replace entire *-bu*, be sure to use *-nde*)
**nomu** -> **nonde** drink (replace entire *-mu*, be sure to use *-nde*)
**shinu** -> **shinde** die (replace entire *-nu*, be sure to use *-nde*)

**tsukuru -> tsukutte** make (replace entire *-ru*, be sure to use *-tte*)

**matsu -> matte** wait (replace entire *-stu*, be sure to use *-tte*)

**harau -> haratte** pay (replace *-u*, be sure to use *-tte*)

*Examples:*

*Hanashite* **kudasai.** Please speak.

*Hanashite* **kaku no wa muzukashii ne.** It's difficult to speak and to write (at the same time), isn't it?

For the past tense, replace *-u* with *-ita* (colloquial) or *-imashita* (polite form):
(types not strictly following the rule, but acting similarly, are listed together)

**hanasu -> hanashita, hanashimashita** talk

**kiku -> kiita** listen (replace entire *-ku*), **kikimashita**

**oyogu -> oyoida** swim (replace entire *-gu*, be sure to use *-ida*), **oyogimashita**

**yobu -> yonda** call (replace entire *-bu*, be sure to use *-nda*), **yobimashita**

**nomu -> nonda** drink (replace entire *-mu*, be sure to use *-nda*), **nomimashita**

**shinu -> shinda** die (replace entire *-nu*, be sure to use *-nda*), **shinimashita**

**tsukuru -> tsukutta** make (replace entire *-ru*, be sure to use *-tta*), **tsukurimashita**

**matsu -> matta** wait (replace entire *-tu*, be sure to use *-tta*), **machimashita**

**harau -> haratta** pay (replace *-u*, be sure to use *-tta*), **haraimashita**

*Examples:*

**Asa ichi jikan denwa-de *hanashita*.** (This) morning (I) chatted on the phone an entire hour.

**Atarashii kompyūtā-ni takusan o-kane wo *haraimashita*.** I paid a lot of money for the new computer.

Replace *-u* with *-itara* for "if" or "when":

This form contains a variety of nuances. It can be used to indicate completed actions, the simple subjunctive, or the conditional. *–tara* is combined with verbs, adjectives and nouns. It can also be used in the subjunctive past perfect: something could have happened, but it didn't.

(types not strictly following the rule, but acting similarly, are grouped)

**hanasu -> hanashitara** talk

**kiku -> kiitara** listen (replace entire *-ku*)

**oyogu -> oyoidara** swim (replace entire *-gu*, be sure to use *-idara*)

**yobu -> yondara** call (replace entire *-bu*, be sure to use *-ndara*)

**nomu -> nondara** drink (replace entire *-mu*, be sure to use *-ndara*)

**shinu -> shindara** die (replace entire *-nu*, be sure to use *-ndara*)

**tsukuru -> tsukuttara** make (replace entire *-ru*, be sure to use *-ttara*)

**matsu** -> **mattara** wait (replace entire *-tu*, be sure to use *-ttara*)

**harau** -> **harattara** pay (replace *-u*, be sure to use *-ttara*)

*Examples:*

**Kare ni sonokoto wo *hanashitara* sugoku okorimashita.** When I told him about it, he got very angry.

**Ano hanashi wo *kiitara* kare-wa konakatta desho.** Had he heard the story, he would not have come.

**Ginko-no rōn wo *harattara* okane wa sukoshishika nokorimasen.** If I pay the bank loan, very little money will be left.

Replace **-u** with *-itari* to indicate several actions following one another or for actions done regularly, in the past:
(types not strictly following the rule, but acting similarly, are listed together)

**hanasu** -> **hanashitari** talk

**kiku** -> **kiitari** listen (replace entire *-ku*)
**oyogu** -> **oyoidari** swim (replace entire *-gu*, be sure to use *-idari*)

**yobu** -> **yondari** call (replace entire *-bu*, be sure to use *-ndari*)
**nomu** -> **nondari** drink (replace entire *-mu*, be sure to use *-ndari*)
**sinu** -> **sindari** die (replace entire *-nu*, be sure to use *-ndari*)
**tsukuru** -> **tsukuttari** make (replace entire *-ru*, be sure to use *-ttari*)

**matsu** -> **mattari** wait (replace entire *-tu*, be sure to use *-ttari*)

**harau** -> **harattari** pay (replace *-u*, be sure to use *-ttari*)

*Examples:*

**Watashitatchi-wa daigaku-de nihongo-wo** *yondari, kaitari, hanashitari* **shimasu.** At university we read, write and speak Japanese.

**Chīsai/chiisai toki-ni kono kawa-de** *oyoidari* **shimashita.** When I was a kid I used to swim in this river.

Replace *-u* with *-eba* for "if" (suffix *-ba* applies to the e-form):

This form expresses a simple condition without any implication of completion of an act. In most situations, *-tara* and *-eba* can be used interchangeably.

**hanasu** -> **hanaseba** talk
**kiku** -> **kikeba** listen
**oyogu** -> **oyogeba** swim
**yobu** -> **yobeba** call
**nomu** -> **nomeba** drink
**sinu** -> **sineba** die
**tsukuru** -> **tsukureba** make
**matsu** -> **mateba** wait
**harau** -> **haraeba** pay

*Examples:*

**O-kyaku-san-ga hayaku** *kaereba,* **watashi-wa eigakan-e ikimasu.** If the guests leave early, I'll go to the movies.

**Hon-wo *yomanakereba* baka-ni narimasu.** If
   one does not read books, one might become
   a fool.

Replace *-u* with *-aseru* for "make (someone) do
something" (causative form):
(regular verb, only one phonetic change in one of
the verb types)

**hanasu** -> **hanasaseru** talk
**kiku** -> **kikaseru** listen
**oyogu** -> **oyogaseru** swim
**yobu** -> **yobaseru** call
**nomu** -> **nomaseru** drink
**sinu** -> **sinaseru** die
**tsukuru** -> **tsukuraseru** make
**matsu** -> **mataseru** wait
**harau** -> **harawaseru** pay

*Example:*
**Okā-san wa kodomo-ni kusuri-wo
   *nomasemashita*.** The mother made the child
   take the medicine.

Replace *-u* with *-areru* for "something that is done
(often to someone)" (passive form):

**hanasu** -> **hanasareru** talk
**kiku** -> **kikareru** listen
**yobu** -> **yobareru** call
**nomu** -> **nomareru** drink
**sinu** -> **sinareru** die
**tsukuru** -> **tsukurareru** make

**matsu -> matareru** wait
**harau -> harawareru** pay

*Examples:*

**Kono sakuhin-wa 100 nen mae-ni**
 ***tsukuraremashita.*** This art was made 100
 years ago.

**Kare-wa tsuma-ni** *shinareta.* He lost his wife.

Replace *-u* with *-aserareru* for "be made to do
something by someone" (causative and passive):

**hanasu -> hanasaserareru** talk
**kiku -> kikaserareru** listen
**oyogu -> oyogaserareru** swim
**yobu -> yobaserareru** call
**nomu -> nomaserareru** drink
**tsukuru -> tsukuraserareru** make
**matsu -> mataserareru** wait
**harau -> harawaserareru** pay (don't forget to
 add *-wa*!)

*Example:*

**Shachō-ni repōto-wo** *kakaserareta.* My boss
 made me write a report for him.

Replace with *-nagara* for concurrent actions:

**Hanashinagara samposhimashita.** (We) talked
 during the walk.

**The Second Inflection: Ru-Verbs**

In ru-verbs, the **ru-** suffix is dropped and/or replaced
by another suffix.

Drop *-ru* and add *-masu*, *-yasui*, etc. (easy to):
**taberu** to eat; **tabemasu** eat; **tabeyasui** easy to eat
**miru** to see; **mimasu** see; **miyasui** easy to see

Replace with *-te* for gerund or simple orders:
**Tabete iku** Eat, then go!
**Are-wo tabete!** Eat that!

Replace with *-ta* or *-mashita* for past tense:
**tabeta, tabemashita** ate
**mita, mimashita** saw

Replace with *-tara* for the meanings "if" or "when" (including subjunctive past, or perfect):
**tabetara** if I/someone eat(s)
**mitara** if I/someone see(s)

*Example:*
*Tabetara* **ikimashō.** When you have finished eating, let's go.

Replace with *-tari* for actions which take place at the same time or shortly after one another:
**Watakushitachi-wa isshoni tabetari nondari shimashita**. We ate and drank together.

Replace with *-reba* for "if":
**mireba** if I/someone see(s)
(This form and the **-tara** form are almost interchangeable.)

Replace with *-yo* for "let's":
**tabeyō** let's eat
**miyō** let's see

Replace with <u>*-ro*</u> for strict orders:
**tabero!** eat!
**miro!** look!

Replace with <u>*-nai*</u> for negative form:
**tabenai** do not eat
**minai** do not look

*Examples:*
**Watashi-wa niku-wo tabenai.** I do not eat meat.
**Watashi-wa terebi-wo minai.** I do not watch TV.

Replace with <u>*–na*</u> for negative command (order):
**tabe runa** do not eat
**miruna** do not look

Replace with <u>*-rareru*</u> for "can" or "be able":
**taberareru** can eat; edible
**Kore taberarenai yo!** I can't eat that!; this is not
   edible

Replace with <u>*-saseru*</u> for "make (someone) do":
**Kore-wo tabesaseyō.** Let's make someone eat this.
**Kore-wo tabesasenai de yo!** Don't make me (or
   anyone else) eat this.

Replace with <u>*-rareru*</u> for passive:
**Kinō kanojo-ni mirareta.** I was seen by her
   yesterday.
**Nezumi-ga neko-ni taberaremashita.** A mouse
   was eaten by a cat.

Replace with *-nagara* for concurrent actions:

**Mado-kara minagara ongaku-wo kikimashita.**

(I) listened to music while looking out of the window.

**Irregular Verbs**

There are only two irregular verbs in Japanese: *suru* (to do) and *kuru* (to come).

**suru** will do *or* does (often, everyday, etc.)
**si** (add *-masu*)
**site** do this (casual command)
**sita** someone did (past tense)
**sitara** if someone does (some connotation of "when")
**sureba** if someone does (no connotation of "when")
**… siyo** let's do …
**siro** do this (rude request)
**sinai** won't do *or* doesn't do (negative)
**sareru** be done (by someone)
**saseru** make (someone) do something
**saserareru** be made to do (by someone)

**kuru** will come *or* comes (often, everyday, etc.)
**ki** (add *-masu*)
**kite** come here (casual command)
**kita** someone came (past tense)
**kitara** if (once) someone comes (some connotation of "when")
**kureba** if someone comes (no connotation of "when")
**koyō** let's come
**koi** come here you (rude request)
**konai** won't come *or* doesn't come (negative)

**korareru** can come
**kosaseru** make (someone) come
**kosaserareru** be made to come (by someone)

### Word Order

The main principle is: SUBJECT - OBJECT - VERB:

**Chizuko-ga hon-wo yomimasu.** Chizuko reads
(*yomimasu*) a book (*hon*).

In more complex sentences the standard word order
when using an active verb is:

(SUBJECT) + TIME + PLACE/IMPLEMENT +
    INDIRECT OBJECT + OBJECT + ACTIVE
    VERB

**(Watashi-wa) ashita daigaku-de tomodachi-ni
hon-wo agemasu.** (I'll) give (*agemasu*) a book
(*hon*) to (my) friend (*tomodachi*) tomorrow
(*ashita*) at the university (*daigaku*).

When using a verb expressing position or existence:

(SUBJECT) + TIME + LOCATION + VERB
    EXPRESSING POSITION OR EXISTENCE

**Chizuko-wa, ima ie-ni iru.** Chizuko is (*iru*) at
home now.
**Chizuko-ga, ima ie-ni iru.** It's Chizuko who is at
home now.

When using verbs of motion the sentence word order is:

(SUBJECT) + TIME + DEPARTURE POINT/ORIGIN + ROUTE + DESTINATION + MOTION VERB

**(Boku-wa) ashita Tōkyō-kara Tōkaidō-wo tōtte Kyōto-e iku.** (I'm) going from Tokyo to Kyoto by the Tokaido road tomorrow.

Subjects are put in parentheses to stress that they are very often omitted. In general, if a new subject is introduced, you have to signal the change by placing *-wa* after the subject. If a subject is clear, but for some reason not omitted (to emphasize, for instance), use *-ga* in order to emphasize the subject, for example:

**(Boku-ga) daijobu ja nai!** I'm not all right!

## ASKING QUESTIONS

The general question is constructed with the verb form *desu* and a particle *-ka*, for example:

Are (you) a student? **(Anata wa) gakusei desu ka?**

The particles are placed at the end of a question. Young people these days usually indicate a question by intonation only: *Gakusei*? (Are you a) student?

The answer is formed by the verb *desu* (when affirmative) or *de wa arimasen* (when negative, full form) or *ja nai* (negative, abbreviated form for casual speech):

Yes, (I'm) a student. **So desu. (Watakushi-wa) gakusei desu.**
No, (I'm) not a student. **Iie. (Watakushi-wa) gakusei de wa arimasen.**
**Ja nai.** [This is] not enough (not good).

which **dono, dochira-no** (polite form)
who **donata, dare**
what **nani**
where **doko, dochira**
how **dōshite, ikani**
which (nt.) **dore**

# THE JAPANESE WRITING SYSTEM

Japanese writing consists of three systems of signs used concurrently in most texts. The first, *kanji*, or Chinese characters, was borrowed from China and consists of ideograms (or hieroglyphs) representing the meaning of a word. There are about two thousand characters used in Japanese texts today.

The Japanese invented two syllabaries based graphically on Chinese characters. Each of them consists of fifty letters. *Katakana*, a phonetic alphabet which is more simple to write and more angular, is primarily used today for writing words borrowed from Western languages and sounds. *Hiragana*, also a phonetic alphabet, is used for original Japanese words and borrowed Chinese words.

# KATAKANA

| | a | ka | sa | ta | na | ha | ma | ya | ra | wa |
|---|---|---|---|---|---|---|---|---|---|---|
| a | ア a | カ ka | サ sa | タ ta | ナ na | ハ ha | マ ma | ヤ ya | ラ ra | ワ wa |
| i | イ i | キ ki | シ shi | チ chi | ニ ni | ヒ hi | ミ mi | | リ ri | |
| u | ウ u | ク ku | ス su | ツ tsu | ヌ nu | フ hu | ム mu | ユ yu | ル ru | |
| e | エ e | ケ ke | セ se | テ te | ネ ne | ヘ he | メ me | | レ re | |
| o | オ o | コ ko | ソ so | ト to | ノ no | ホ ho | モ mo | ヨ yo | ロ ro | ヲ wo |
| | | | | | | | | | | ン n |

# HIRAGANA

| | | | | | | | | | | |
|---|---|---|---|---|---|---|---|---|---|---|
| あ a | か ka | さ sa | た ta | な na | は ha | ま ma | や ya | ら ra | わ wa | |
| い i | き ki | し shi | ち chi | に ni | ひ hi | み mi | | り ri | | |
| う u | く ku | す su | つ tsu | ぬ nu | ふ hu | む mu | ゆ yu | る ru | | |
| え e | け ke | せ se | て te | ね ne | へ he | め me | | れ re | | |
| お o | こ ko | そ so | と to | の no | ほ ho | も mo | よ yo | ろ ro | を wo | ん n |

# PRONUNCIATION GUIDE

| Transliteration | Approximate English Equivalent |
|---|---|
| a | father |
| i | machine |
| u | put |
| e | bet |
| o | horse |
| k before a, u, e, o | coot |
| k before i, and ky | cute |
| s before a, u, e, o | see |
| sh before i and shy | between *sh* in **she** and *s* in **see** (closer to *s*) |
| t before a, e, o | tip |
| t turns *ch* before i and chy | between *ch* in **cheap** and *t* in **tip** |
| t turns *ts* before u | **ts**etse fly |
| n before a, u, e, o | deny |
| n before i and ny | me**n**u or ave**n**ue |
| h before a, e, o | **h**ot |
| h before i and hy | **h**umid |
| m before a, u, e, o | re**m**ind |
| m before i and my | a**m**use |
| r before a, u, e, o | very |
| z | ol**d z**ebra |

Japanese letters *ki, shi, chi, ni, ri* with small letters *ya, yu and yo* behind them (き ゃ, き ゅ, き ょ ,etc.) indicate palatalized consonants and should read *kya, kyu, kyo*, etc. without making a break between consonant and vowel.

Two small parallel lines at the upper right side of letter in rows *k, s, t, h* (ガ, ギ, グ, ゲ, ゴ, etc.) indicate their full-voiced correspondences: *g, z, d, b*.

A small round sign at the upper right corner of letters in a *h*-row (パ, ピ, プ) indicates that these syllables should begin with *p*.

The letter *u* (う ) after a syllable ending with *o* or *u* indicates a long vowel. For example, そ and う read *soo*. In academic Romanization long vowels are designated by a macron sign above the letter *o* or *u*.

The object marker **wo**, which appears (hyphenated) after nouns, should be read like *o*.

# JAPANESE-ENGLISH DICTIONARY

## A

**aida** between; during
**ai-suru** to love
**aisu tii** iced tea
**aji** saurel
**akabō** porter
**akabudōshu** red wine
**aka-chan** baby
**akai** red (adj.)
**akakabu** radish
**aki** autumn
**amagumo** rain cloud
**amai** sweet (adj.)
**amari** much; many
**ame** rain
**amerika-jin** American
**ampuru** ampoule
**an** project; plan
**anago** conger eel
**anata** you (sg.)
**anatagata** you (pl.)
**ane** older sister
**ani** older brother
**annaijō** information desk
**annaisho** guidebook
**ano** that (adj.)
**anohito** that person (all genders)
**anzu** apricot
**aoi** blue (adj.)
**apāto** apartment

**arashi** storm
**are** that (n.)
**arigatō** thank you
**aru** to be
**arukōru** alcohol
**aruku** to walk
**asa** morning
**asatte** day after tomorrow
**aseru** to be nervous
**ashi** leg; foot
**ashita** tomorrow
**asupirin** aspirin
**atama** head
**atatakai** warm
**atena** address
**ato** after
**atsui** hot
**au** to meet
**ayamaru** to apologize
**ayame** iris

# B

**bā** bar
**ba** place
**bāgen** bargain
**baiorin** violin
**baiten** kiosk; newsstand
**bajutsu** horseback riding
**baka** fool; foolish; stupid
**bakabakashii** foolish
**bamen** scene (part of performance)

**banchi** building number
**bangō** number
**barē** ballet
**basu** bus
**basukettobōru** basketball
**basu-rūmu** bathroom
**batā** butter
**benkyō-suru** to study
**biiru** beer
**bijutsu** art
**binsen** letter paper
**biru** building
**biyōin** beauty parlor
**bōhū** hurricane
**bōken** adventure; risk
**bōkō** bladder
**bokushi** priest
**bokusingu** boxing
**budō** grape
**budōshu** wine
**bun** part; fragment
**bungaku** literature
**bungei** art and literature
**bunka** culture
**bunka-kōryū** cultural exchange
**bunshō** sentence
**buta** pig
**butai** stage (place of performance)
**butaniku** pork
**butsuri (gaku)** physics
**byo** second (n.)
**byōin** hospital
**byōki** illness

## C

**cha (o-cha)** tea
**chairo** brown (n.)
**chesu** chess
**chi** blood
**chichi** father
**chichioya** father
**chigau** to be wrong; to be different
**chiisai** small
**chiizu** cheese
**chikadō** underground walkway
**chikagai** underground shopping area
**chikai** close; near
**chikatetsu** subway
**chinseizai** tranquilizer
**chirigaku** geography
**chiryō** medical treatment
**chizu** map; plan
**chosha** author
**chotto** a little
**chōzō** statue (stone)
**chūdoku** poisoning
**chūō** center
**chūsha** injection
**chūshaki** syringe

## D

**dabokushō** bruise (n.)
**dai** big; large
**daidokoro** kitchen
**daikon** (white) horseradish

**daigaku** college; university
**dai-go-no** fifth
**dai-hachi-no** eighth
**daihyōdan** delegation
**dai-ichi-no** first (adj.)
**daijōbu** all right
**dai-ju ichi-no** eleventh
**dai-ju-no** tenth
**daikon** white radish
**dai-kyū-no** ninth
**dai-ni-no** second (adj.)
**dai-roku-no** sixth
**dai-san-no** third
**dai-shichi-no** seventh
**daisū** algebra
**dai-yon-no** fourth
**danshihuku** men's apparel
**danshiyō-sūtsu** men's suit
**dare** who
**deguchi** exit
**dekiru** to be able
**dempō** telegram
**dendōkan** mission
**dendōshi** preacher
**denki** electricity
**denkiya** electric appliance store
**densenbyō** infectious/epidemic disease
**densetsu** legend
**densha** tram; train
**denshi-meiru** e-mail
**dentō** lamp
**denwa** telephone
**denwachō** telephone directory

**depāto** department store
**disuko** disco
**dōbutsu** animal(s)
**dōbutsu-gakusha** zoologist
**dochira** who (polite form)
**Doitsu** Germany
**dōjō** sympathy; consolation
**dokuritsu** independence
**dokushin** single (not married)
**dōmo** very much
**dōmyaku-koka** sclerosis
**dono** which (possessive form)
**dore** which
**doresu** dress
**dorobō** robbery
**doyōbi** Saturday
**dōzo** please
**dōzō** statue (bronze)


# E

**e** picture; drawing
**eakon** air conditioner
**ebi** shrimp
**eda** branch
**ee** yes
**eiga** cinema
**eigakan** movie theater
**eigyōchū** open (restaurant)
**Eikoku** Great Britain
**Eiwa** English-Japanese
**eki** station; terminal
**ekiin** station officer

**empitsu** pencil

**en** yen

**engeki** drama (art)

**erebētā** elevator

**esukarētā** escalator

**etsuran** reading

**etsuran-kādo** library card

**etsuran-shitsu** reading room

# F
*(occurs in imported words only)*

**fakkusu** fax

**fan** fan

**fiito** foot (measure)

**firumu** film

**fōku** fork

**Furansu** France

**furonto-gakari** receptionist (front desk)

# G

**gaidobukku** guidebook

**gaijin** foreigner

**gaikokujin** foreigner

**gaka** artist

**gakki** instrument

**gakki** semester

**gakkō** school

**gakubu** faculty (division)

**gakudan** orchestra

**gakui** academic degree
**gakuin** institute
**gakureki** education (history)
**gakusha** scholar
**gakushi** college graduate (bachelor's degree)
**gambatte!** go for it!
**garon** gallon
**gawa** side
**geijutsu** art
**geinōjin** entertainer (unisex)
**geka** surgery
**geki** play; drama
**gekidan** theater (troupe)
**gekijō** theater (building)
**gekisakka** dramatist; playwright
**gendai** contemporary
**gengogaku** linguistics
**genki** (good) health
**genkin** cash
**genkō** original (not a translation)
**gesha-suru** to get off
**geta** traditional Japanese sandals
**getsuyōbi** Monday
**gichōdan** presidium
**gihu** stepfather
**gikyoku** play
**gin** silver
**ginkō** bank
**gitā** guitar
**go** five
**gogatsu** May
**gogo** afternoon
**gojū** fifty

**gomen** apology
**gozen** before noon
**guramu** gram
**guriin-sha** first-class car in a train ("green car")
**gyō** line
**gyūniku** beef
**gyūnyū** milk

# H

**ha** tooth/teeth
**hachi** eight
**hachigatsu** August
**hachijū** eighty
**hadagi** underwear
**hagaki** postcard
**hageshii** violent; acute
**haguki** gum
**hahaoya** mother
**hai** lung
**hai** yes
**haien** pneumonia
**haiku** poem of 17 syllables
**haitatsu-shōmei yūbin** certified letter
**haiyū** actor; actress
**haizara** ashtray
**haji** shame
**hakase** doctor (Ph.D., M.D.)
**hakubutsukan** museum
**hakumai** rice (white)
**hambāgu** hamburger
**hamu** ham

**han** half
**hana** flower
**hana** nose
**hanashi** talk (n.); speech
**hanasu** to speak
**hanemūn** honeymoon
**hanga** print (engraving, block print)
**hara** belly; abdomen
**harako** roe
**hare** clear; fine
**hari** needle
**haru** spring
**hashi** bridge
**hashi** chopsticks
**hataraku** to work
**hatsubai** sale
**hatsugen-suru** to speak (at a meeting or a conference)
**hatsuka-kan** twenty days
**hayai** early; soon
**henji** answer (n.)
**heya** room
**hi** sun; fire
**hibun** inscription
**hidari** left
**hidoi** very bad
**hige** facial hair
**higeki** tragedy
**higure** twilight
**hihu** skin
**hiirō** hero
**hiji** elbow

**hijōji** emergency
**hikōki** airplane
**hiku** to play (string and keyed instruments)
**hima** leisure
**hinode** sunrise
**hinyōki** urinary organs
**hiraku** to open
**hirame** flounder
**hiroba** square; circle
**hiru** daytime (as opposed to night)
**hisshū** compulsory; required
**hitai** forehead
**hito** one person (all genders)
**hitobito** people; they
**hitori** one person; alone
**hitotsu** one
**hiza** knee
**hōgakubu** law school
**hōmu** platform
**hon** book
**hone** bone
**hontō** really
**honya** bookstore
**honyaku** translation (action)
**honyakusho** translation (book)
**hōritsu** law
**hoshi** star
**hōtai** bandage
**hotategai** scallop
**hoteru** hotel (western-style)
**hotoke-sama** buddha
**hude** brush (n.)
**hujin** woman

**hujinfuku** ladies' apparel
**hukai** deep
**hukō** unhappiness
**hukōna** bad; terrible; unhappy
**hukuinsho** Gospel
**hun** minute
**hurudō gu ya** second-hand store
**husagaru** to be full; to be occupied; to be choked;
    to be busy
**hushigina** strange
**hushō** wound
**hutatsu** two
**hūtō** envelope
**hutsū** usual; common; local (train)
**hutsuka yoi** hangover
**huyu** winter
**hyakka-jiten** encyclopedia
**hyaku** hundred
**hyakuman** million
**hyōdai** title
**hyōshi** cover


# I

**i** stomach
**ichi** one
**ichiban** first; the best
**ichido** once
**ichigatsu** January
**ichinenkan** one year
**ichinichi** one day
**ie** house; home
**igaku** medical science

**igakusha** physician (scholar)

**Igirisu** United Kingdom

**ii** good

**iie** no

**ii-meiru** e-mail

**ika** cuttlefish; squid

**i-kataru** gastritis

**ike** pond; lake

**ikkagetsukan** one month

**iku** to go; to come

**ikura** red (salmon) roe

**ima** now

**imi** meaning

**imōto** younger sister

**inkina** gloomy

**inori** prayer

**insatsu-shiryō** printed materials

**inu** dog

**ippai** to be full

**iriguchi** entrance

**iro** color

**iroppoi** sexy; seductive

**irui** clothes

**isha** physician; doctor

**isogashii** busy

**issakujitsu** the day before yesterday

**isshōkemmei** with all (my, your) might

**isshūkan** one week

**Isuraeru** Israel

**isuraeru-jin** Israeli

**itadaku** to accept

**Itaria** Italy

**itasu** to do (*only the 1st person, very polite way to speak to a senior person*)

**i-tsu** stomachache
**itsu** when
**itsutsu** five
**iu** to tell; to speak
**iwashi** sardine
**iya-na** disgusting
**izakaya** drinking parlor; bar


# J

**jazu** jazz
**ji** hour
**jibiinkōka** otolaryngology
**jiin** monastery (Buddhist)
**jiinzu** jeans
**jikan** time
**jikokuhyō** timetable
**jimukyoku** secretariat
**jimusho** office
**jinja** Shintoist shrine
**jinkō** population
**jintai** (human) body
**jinzo** kidney
**jishin** earthquake
**jiten** dictionary
**jitensha** bicycle
**jiyū** freedom
**jobun** foreword
**jōhō** data
**joyū** actress
**jōzai** pills
**jōzu-na** skillful
**JR** Japan Railway (a railway company)

**jū** ten
**jūdō** judo
**jūgatsu** October
**jugyū** lesson; lecture
**jūichigatsu** November
**jūman** hundred thousand
**junbichū** closed (stores, restaurants)
**jūnigatsu** December
**jūsho** address
**jūsu** juice
**jūtaku** residence
**jutsu** skill (n.)


# K

**kaban** bag
**kabu** turnip
**kado** street corner
**kaeru** frog
**kaeru** to return
**kagaku** chemistry
**kagi** key
**kagu** furniture
**kaidan** stairs
**kaiga** painting
**kaigaten** picture exhibition
**kaigi** conference
**kaikei** accounting; cashier
**kaikeigakari** accountant
**kaisha** firm; company
**kaisōroku** memoirs
**kaki** persimmon
**kakitome yūbin** registered letter

**kakkoii** cool
**kaku** to write
**kamera** camera
**kamera'ya** photo shop
**kameraman** cameraman
**kami** paper
**kami** Shintoist deities
**kamoku** course (discipline)
**kamukōdā** camcorder
**kanai** wife
**kanashii** sad
**kangaeru** to think
**kangohu** nurse
**kani** crab
**kanjō** service bill
**kanjōgaki** bill of services
**kankyaku** viewer
**kannushi** Shinto priest
**kanojo** she
**kanran** viewing
**kantoku** (film) director
**kanzō** liver
**kanzume** canned (usually food)
**kao** face
**karada** body
**karai** spicy; hot
**karate** karate
**kare** he
**karē-raisu** rice with curry
**karifurawā** cauliflower
**kasumi** haze
**kata** shoulder
**katachi** image
**katagawa** one side

**katamichi** one way
**kau** to buy
**kawa** leather
**kawa** river
**kawaii** cute
**kayōbi** Tuesday
**kayui** to be itchy
**kazan** volcano
**kaze** wind
**kazoku** family
**kedo** but; so
**kega-wo suru** to be injured
**keikan** policeman
**kekko** good; enough; correct
**kekkon** marriage
**kekkon-shiki** wedding ceremony
**kekkon-suru** to marry
**kembutsu** sightseeing
**kenchiku** architecture
**kenkyujo** research institute; lab
**kensa** test
**keredo** but; so
**keredomo** but; so
**keshiki** landscape
**keshōshitsu** toilet ("powder room")
**kesshōten** finish; goal
**ki** spirit
**ki** tree
**kibishii** harsh
**kigeki** comedy
**kikagaku** geometry
**kiken** danger
**kiko** climate

**kiku** chrysanthemum
**kiku** to hear; to listen
**kimi** you (informal)
**kimmusaki** working place (usually company name)
**kimochi** feeling; (in slang): good; pleasant
**kin'en** no smoking
**kin'yōbi** Friday
**kinniku** muscle
**ki-no ko** mushrooms
**kinō** yesterday
**kinu** silk
**kion** air temperature
**kippu** ticket
**kippu uriba** ticket box
**kirei-na** beautiful
**kiri** mist; fog
**kiro, kiromētoru** kilometer
**kiroguramu** kilogram
**kiroku** record (memo, a note)
**kiroku** record (sport)
**kiroku-wo tsukuru** to set a record (sport)
**kisetsu** season
**kisha** train
**kisha-kaiken** press conference
**kishi** bank; shore
**kisu** kiss (n.)
**kitsune** fox
**kōban** police station (post)
**kōcha** black tea
**kōdō** lecture hall; auditorium
**kodomo** child/children
**kodomofuku** children's apparel
**koe** voice
**kōen** park

**kōgi** lecture
**kohada** gizzard shad
**kōhii** coffee
**koi** strong (coffee, tea)
**kōjō** factory
**kōjō** plant, fauna (n.)
**kōka** coin(s)
**koka-kōra** coca cola
**kokonotsu** nine
**kokoro** heart
**kōkūbin** airmail (letter)
**kokumin** citizen
**kokuseki** nationality
**kokyō** motherland
**kōkyō-gakudan** symphony orchestra
**komaru** to experience difficulties; to be puzzled
**kompyūtā** computer
**kone** contact, connection
**kon'yakku** cognac
**kongetsu** this month
**kono** this (adj.)
**konshū** this week
**konsome** bouillon
**koppu** glass (of wine, beer, etc.)
**kore** this (closer to speaker)
**kōri** ice
**kōryū** exchange (of culture and ideas)
**kōsaten** intersection
**kōsei-busshitsu** antibiotics
**koshi** waist
**koshō** out of order; not working
**koten** classic literature
**kōtō kyōiku** higher education (usually college and
  above)

**koto** matter
**kotoshi** this year
**kotowaza** proverb
**kotozuke** message
**kowai** fearful
**kōzui** flood
**kozutsumi** parcel
**ku** area; city district
**ku** nine
**kuchi** mouth
**kuchibiru** lip
**kudamono** fruit
**kudamonoya** greengrocer
**kudasai** please
**kugatsu** September
**kūkō** airport
**kuma** bear
**kumo** cloud
**kumori** cloudy
**kure** end of…(year, etc.)
**kuriiningu** laundry
**kuroi** black; dark
**kuru** to come
**kuruma** car
**kuruma ebi** prawn
**kusuri** medicine
**kusuriya** drugstore; pharmacy
**kutsu** shoes
**kyabetsu** cabbage
**kyabia** caviar
**kyaku** guest
**kyakuma** guest room

**kyapten** captain
**kyasshu kōnā** ATM ('cash corner')
**kyō** today
**kyōdai** siblings
**kyōju** professor
**kyōkaidō** church
**kyōkan** instructor (very formal)
**kyōkasho** textbook; manual
**kyōmi** interest
**kyonen** last year
**kyōshitsu** classroom
**kyōsō** competition (running or other)
**kyōsō** racing
**kyōzai** educational materials
**kyūjū** ninety
**kyūkō** express
**kyūkyūsha** ambulance
**kyūri** cucumber


# M

**ma** space
**machi** town block
**machi** town; city
**machiaishitsu** waiting hall
**machigau** to be wrong
**made** till; to
**madoguchi** office window
**mae** before
**mae-no** in front of
**magaru** to turn

**mago** (unisex) grandson; granddaughter

**magomusume** granddaughter

**maguro** tuna

**mairu** mile

**mairu** to come (*1st person*)

**makuai** intermission

**mamahaha** stepmother

**mamako** stepchild

**man** ten thousand (one *man*)

**manabu** to study (a subject)

**mandan** repartee

**manējā** manager

**manga** comics

**marason** marathon

**masaka** surely not

**massugu** straight

**mata** again; and

**matsu** pine tree

**matsu** to wait

**mayonaka** midnight

**mazui** bad taste; tasteless

**me** eye

**mēdo-san** maid

**megane** glasses

**meisō** meditation

**meitei** drunkenness

**meitengai** street with many stores

**meron** melon

**mētoru** meter

**michi** road; way; path

**midori** green

**migi** right

**mihon** sample

**mikan** tangerine

**minashigo** orphan

**mingei** folk

**miru** to look; to see

**miruku** milk

**miseru** to show

**mittsu** three

**mizore** sleet

**mizu** water

**mochiron** of course

**mōchōen** appendicitis

**mōichido** once more

**mokuji** contents

**mokuyōbi** Thursday

**momo** peach

**mono** thing

**monogatari** stories

**morau** to ask for something (*1st person asking 2nd person*)

**mori** forest

**motto** more

**mottomo** very (superlative)

**mune** breast

**murasaki** violet; lilac

**muri** impossible

**muryō** free (no charge)

**mushiatsui** muggy

**musuko** son

**musume** daughter

**muttsu** six

**myōgonichi** the day after tomorrow

# N

**naganegi** scallion
**naifu** knife
**naika** internal medicine
**nakusu** to lose
**namae** name
**nana** seven
**nanatsu** seven
**nani** what
**naosu** to correct; to repair
**napukin** napkin
**naru** to become
**naruhodo** indeed
**nashi** pear
**natsu** summer
**nedan** price
**neko** cat
**nemui** sleepy
**nemuru** to sleep
**nengō** calendar era
**nenkan** yearbook
**nenrei** age
**netsu** temperature; fever
**ni** two
**nibui** slow; dull; dim
**nichi** day (24 hours)
**nichibotsu** sunset
**nichiyōbi** Sunday
**nigai** bitter
**niganigashii** shameful
**nigatena** not good at
**nigatsu** February

**nijū** twenty
**nikai** 2nd floor
**nikaiseki** balcony (in a theater)
**niku** meat
**nimotsu** luggage
**ninjin** carrot
**ninniku** garlic
**nishin** herring
**nittei** day's schedule; itinerary
**no** field
**nodo-ga kawaku** to be thirsty
**noikketsu** cerebral hemorrhage
**nomimono** drink(s)
**nomu** to drink
**nori** glue; laver (seaweed)
**norikae** transfer (of buses, trains)
**norikaeru** to make a transfer
**norimono** means of transportation
**noru** to get aboard
**nōto** notebook
**nyūgaku** to enter (university)
**nyūjōryō** entrance fee


## O

**oba** aunt
**ōbākōto** overcoat
**o-bāsan** grandma
**o-bōsan** Buddhist priest
**ōdan-hodō** street crossing
**odori** dance
**odoroku** to be surprised

**ōhuku** round trip (ticket)

**oishii** delicious

**oji** uncle

**ojiisan** grandpa

**o-kane** money

**ōkii** big

**oku** one hundred millions (*one* oku)

**okubyō-mono** coward

**okuru** to send

**okusan** wife (*of the* $2^{nd}$ *and* $3^{rd}$ *person*)

**o-mikuji** oracle

**omosa** weight

**omou** to think

**ongaku** music

**onna** woman

**onsu** ounce

**Oranda** Holland; Dutch

**orenji** orange (n.)

**oriibu oiru** olive oil

**orugan** organ (instrument)

**oshieru** to explain

**osoi** late

**Ōsutoraria** Australia

**o-tearai** toilet ("hand-washing place")

**oto** sound

**otogi-banashi** fairy tale

**otoko** man

**otona** adult

**o-tōsan** father

**otōto** younger brother

**ototoi** the day before yesterday

**otto** husband (general term)

**o-yatsu** snacks; refreshment

**oyogi** swimming
**oyogu** to swim

## P

**pabu** pub
**pachinko** gambling machine
**painappuru** pineapple
**pan** bread
**pan'ya** bakery
**pāsento** percent
**pēji** page
**pen** pen
**piano** piano
**piru** contraceptive pills
**pondo** pound
**posuto** mailbox (postal)
**poteto** potato
**puresu-sentā** press center
**puroguramingu** programming

## R

**raigetsu** next month
**raihin** guest(s)
**rainen** next year
**raishu** next week
**raisu** rice
**rapputoppu kompyūtā** laptop computer
**rasshu awā** rush hour

**referii** referee
**rei** zero
**reibo** air conditioning
**reihaishiki** (religious) service
**rejii** cashier
**rekishī** history
**rekishika** historian
**remon** lemon
**renga** poem of linked verse
**renkōto** raincoat
**renraku** communication; contacts
**renraku-suru** to contact
**rentogen** X ray
**repātorii** repertoire
**ressha** train
**resuringu** wrestling
**retsu** line
**rikon** divorce
**rikon-suru** to divorce
**ringo** apple
**risaikuru shoppu** second-hand store
**rittoru** liter
**rōdōsha** worker; laborer
**rokku-n-rōru** rock-n-roll
**roku** six
**rokugatsu** June
**rokujū** sixty
**rokumakuen** pleurisy
**rombun** article; paper; thesis
**Roshia** Russia
**ryōjikan** consulate
**ryokan** hotel (Japanese-style)
**ryokōsha** travel agency
**ryōshin** parents

**ryōshūsho** receipt
**ryūkan** influenza

## S

**saba** mackerel
**sabi** antique look
**saigai** natural disaster
**saihu** wallet
**saiketsu-suru** to vote
**sainan** disaster
**sakana** fish
**sakaya** liquor store
**sake** sake (Japanese rice wine)
**sakebu** to shout
**saki** in front of; before
**sakkā** (European) football; soccer
**sakka** writer
**sakkyokuka** composer
**sakuhin** literary piece
**sakuhinshū** complete works (books)
**sakura** cherry
**sama** (more polite form of *san*, unisex) Mr.; Mrs.
**sambun** prose
**samui** cold
**san** (unisex) polite suffix used after person's name
**san** three
**sandoitchi** sandwich
**sangatsu** March
**sanjū** thirty
**sanretsu-suru** to participate (ceremonies)
**sappari** totally

**sara** plate
**saru** monkey
**sashimi** sliced raw fish (dish)
**satō** sugar
**sawaru** to disturb; to touch
**sayōnara** good-bye
**sebiro** men's suit
**seibutsugaku** biology
**seigaku** vocal music
**seihu** government
**seikeigeka** plastic surgery
**seikyūhyo** order slip (in a library)
**seimei** surname and given name
**seisanjo** fare adjustment machine (train station)
**seisho** Bible
**seishokuki** genitals
**seishokusha** priest
**seki** seat
**sekiri** dysentery
**sekkyo** sermon
**sen** thousand
**senaka** back (n.)
**senchimētoru** centimeter
**sengetsu** last month
**senkyōshi** missionary
**senmenjo** toilet ("washroom")
**senmon** specialty
**sensei** teacher; advisor doctor (polite form of address)
**senshū** last week
**senshu** sportsman (in a competition)
**senshuken-taikai** championship
**sentaku** choice
**sentaku** laundry (washing)

**sēru** on sale
**sētā** sweater
**setsumei** explanation; instruction
**setsumeisho** manual
**shabu-shabu** slices of beef dipped in boiling water
**shakai** society
**shakaigaku** sociology
**shamisen** traditional 3-string musical instrument
**shampan** champagne; sparkling wine
**shashinten** photography exhibit
**shashō** conductor (in train)
**shi** four
**shiai** match
**shibai** performance (of a play)
**shibori** wet towel
**shibui** chic
**shichi** seven
**shichijū** seventy
**shichigatsu** July
**shigatsu** April
**shigoto** job; work (n.)
**shigoto-wo suru** to work
**shihei** bill (banknote)
**shijin** poet
**shika-i** dentist
**shikashi** but
**shiken** exam (in school)
**shiken-ni ochiru** to fail an exam
**shiken-ni pasu-suru** to pass an exam
**shikisha** conductor (music)
**shima** island
**shimai** sister(s)
**shimau** to complete; finish
**shimbun** newspaper

**shimeru** to close (doors)

**shimo** frost

**shindaisha** sleeping car

**shingenchi** epicenter

**shinkei** nerve

**shinkeitsu** neuralgia

**shinpai** anxiety

**shinrin-kanshiin** forest ranger

**shinsatsu** examination (medical)

**shinseki** relative

**shinshitsu** bedroom

**shinzō** heart

**shinzōbyō** heart failure

**shio** salt

**shiri** buttocks

**shirobudōshu** white wine

**shiroi** white (adj.)

**shiru** to know

**shisai** Orthodox Christian priest

**shishobako** post office box (P.O.B.)

**shita** tongue

**shiteiken** ticket (reserved seat)

**shiten** branch (of office)

**shitsudo** humidity

**shizuka** quiet

**shō** chapter

**shō** ministry

**shōchi** agreement

**shōga** ginger

**shōgo** midday; noon

**shohōsen** prescription

**shōjō** symptoms

**shokudō** dining room

**shokudōsha** restaurant car

**shokugyō** occupation; profession

**shokuryohin'ya** grocery

**shokuseki** position (in a company)

**shōnika** pediatrics

**shoppingu sentā** shopping mall

**shosai** study room

**shoseki** book in general

**shosekiten** book exhibition

**shōsetsu** novel

**shōtaigawa** hosting

**shoten** bookstore

**shūdōin** monastery; convent (Christian)

**shūdōsō** monk

**shuha** sect

**shuhu** housewife

**shujin** husband (*of the 1st person*)

**shujutsu** surgery

**shukudai** homework

**shuppansha** publishing house

**shuppatsu** departure

**shyūkyō** religion

**simfonii** symphony

**simpojiumu** symposium

**sirubā-siito** seat for the elderly and disabled ("silver seat")

**soba** buckwheat noodle

**soba** nearby

**sōdankai** consultation

**sōjūshi** pilot

**sokkusu** socks

**sokutatsu** special delivery (express mail)

**sono** this (adj.)

**sora** sky

**sore** this (n.)

**sorera** they (not human beings)

**sōsēji** sausage

**sotsugyō** graduation

**sōzōshii** noisy

**subarashii** splendid; beautiful

**sūgaku** mathematics

**sūgakusha** mathematician

**sugoi** awesome; terrific

**suiei** swimming

**suika** watermelon

**suion** water temperature

**suiyōbi** Wednesday

**sukāto** skirt

**sukēto kyogi** skating competition

**suki** to like

**sukiyaki** meat and vegetables in soy sauce

**sukoshi** a little

**sumimasen** sorry; excuse me

**sumō** sumo wrestling

**sumomo** plum (fruit)

**sunpō** measure

**sūpā (māketto)** supermarket

**supōtsu** sports

**suppai** sour

**supūn** spoon

**surippa** slippers

**sushiya** sushi bar

**sutāto** start

**sutēki** steak

# T

**o-tera** Buddhist temple
**o-tsuri** change (money)
**tabemono** food
**taberu** to eat
**tabi** Japanese socks
**tabun** probably
**taihen** great; much
**taihū** typhoon
**taiiku** athletics
**taikai** congress
**taiki** air; atmosphere
**taisetsu** importance
**taishikan** embassy
**taisō** gymnastics
**takai** expensive; high
**take** bamboo
**tako** octopus
**tamago** egg
**tamanegi** onion
**tāminaru** terminal
**tampakkusu** tampon
**tampen-shōsetsu** short story
**tanjōbi** birthday
**tanka** poem of 31 syllables
**tanoshii** pleasant; jovial; cheerful
**tanuki** badger
**tariru** be enough
**tasogare** twilight
**tatemono** building
**tateru** to build
**te** hand
**tegami** letter

**teire** maintenance
**teiryūjo** (bus) stop
**tēma** theme
**ten'in** salesperson
**tenjikan** pavilion
**tenki** weather
**tennō** (Japanese) emperor
**tenrankai** exhibition
**terebi** television
**tiimu** team
**tō** bell tower
**tō** ten
**tobikomu** to jump in
**tōchaku** arrival
**toire** toilet
**tokei** watch; clock
**tokka** special price (sale)
**tokkyū** special express (train)
**tokoya** barber
**tomato** tomato
**tomeru** to stop
**tonari** next to
**tōnyōbyō** diabetes
**tooi** far
**toori** street
**tooru** to follow
**toraberāzu chekku** traveler's check
**torēnā** trainer
**tori** bird
**torikaeru** to exchange
**tōroku** registration
**toshi** year
**toshokan** library

**totemo** very

**tōyaku** medication

**tozan** rock climbing

**tsū** pain

**tsugi** next

**tsukareru** to be tired

**tsuki** month

**tsuki** moon

**tsukue** table

**tsuma** wife (*general term*)

**tsuman'nai** boring

**tsumetai** cold; chilly

**tsumi** guilt

**tsumori** intention

**tsūshin** communication

**tsutome** job

**tsutsumu** wrap up

**tsūyaku** interpretation

**tsuyoi** strong

**tsuyu** dew


## U

**ubu** naive; innocent

**ude** arm

**udon** noodles

**uketsuke** information desk

**umai** delicious (m.)

**ume** plum tree (or fruit)

**unagi** eel

**untenshu** driver

**uokka** vodka

**ureshii** glad; enjoy
**ushiro** behind
**usui** thin, weak (coffee, tea)
**uta** classical Japanese poem
**utai** song (classic Japanese)
**utau** to sing
**utsukushii** beautiful
**uwagi** jacket


# W

**wabi** apology
**wadai** subject of conversation
**wahuku** Japanese clothing
**wain** wine
**wakai** young
**wakaru** to understand
**wake** meaning
**wakibara** side
**warui** bad
**wasabi** (green) horseradish
**washiki** Japanese style
**watakushi** I
**watakushitachi** we
**wataru** to cross (a street)


# Y

**ya** shop
**yaburu** to break; tear
**yachin** rent (n.)

**yado** accommodation

**yakamashii** noisy; pestering

**yake** despair

**yakitori** grilled chicken

**yakusha** actor; actress

**yakusho** (government) office

**yakusho** translation

**yakyū** baseball

**yama** mountain

**Yamato** ancient name of Japan

**yasai** vegetables

**yasashii** easy; kind

**yasui** cheap

**yasumi** rest; break

**yasumu** to rest

**yattsu** eight

**yawaraka** tender; sweet; soft

**yōbi** days of the week

**yohō** forecast

**yōhuku** Western clothing

**yōhukuya** clothing store

**yoi** good

**yokin** bank deposit

**yomu** to read

**yōniku** lamb; mutton

**yonjū** forty

**yoroshii** good

**yoru** night

**yōshi** adopted child (male)

**yōshiki** Western style

**yottsu** four

**you** to get drunk

**yubi** finger

**yūbin** mail (n.)
**yūbinkyoku** post office
**yue** reason
**yūei-suru** to swim leisurely
**yūgata** evening
**yukata** summer kimono
**yuketsu** blood transfusion
**yuki** snow
**yukidoke** thaw (snow)
**yukkuri** slowly
**yuku** to go
**yume** dream
**yūmei** famous; popular
**yūmoa** humor
**yurusu** to let; to permit; to pardon


## Z

**zabuton** sitting mat (cushion)
**zadan** idle chat
**zaijū** to live in a foreign country
**zannen** regret
**zasshi** journal; magazine
**zazen** meditation
**zemināru** seminar
**zenkei** panoramic view
**zettai** absolutely
**zō** portrait
**zōge** ivory
**zōri** sandals
**zōsho** library (private)
**zubon** pants

# ENGLISH-JAPANESE DICTIONARY

## A

**abdomen** hara
**able (to be)** dekiru
**absolutely** zettai; mattaku
**academic degree** gakui
**accept** itadaku
**accommodation** yado
**accountant** kaikeigakari
**accounting** kaikei
**actor** danyū (m.); (all genders) geinōjin; haiyu;
    yakusha
**actress** joyū
**acute** hageshii
**address** (n.) atena; jūsho
**adopted child** yōshi (m.); yojō (f.)
**adult** otona
**adventure** bōken
**advisor** kyōkan
**aerogram** hūkanhagaki
**after** ato; ushiro
**afternoon** gogo
**after tomorrow** myōgonichi
**again** mata
**age** (n.) nenrei
**agreement** shōchi
**air conditioner** ea-kon
**air** kūki
**airmail** kōkūbin
**airplane** hikōki
**airport** kūkō

**air temperature** kion
**alcohol** arukōru
**algebra** daisū
**a little** chotto; sukoshi
**all right** daijōbu
**alone** hitori
**ambulance** kyūkyūsha
**American** amerika-jin
**ampoule** ampuru
**and** mata
**animals** dōbutsu
**answer** (n.) henji
**antibiotics** kōsei-busshitsu
**antique look** sabi
**anxiety** shimpai
**apartment** apāto; jūtaku
**apology** gomen; shitsurei; wabi
**appendicitis** mōchōen
**apple** ringo
**apricot** anzu
**April** shigatsu
**architecture** kenchiku
**area** ku
**arm** ude
**arrival** tōchaku
**art** geijutsu
**art and literature** bungei
**article** rombun; kiji
**artist** gaka (painter)
**ashtray** haizara
**ask something** (*1st person asking the 2nd*) morau
**aspirin** asupirin

**athletics** taiiku
**ATM** kyasshu kōnā ("cash corner")
**atmosphere** taiki
**auditorium** kyōshitsu, kōdō
**August** hachigatsu
**aunt** oba
**Australia** Ōsutoraria
**author** chosha
**autumn** aki
**awesome** sugoi


# B

**baby** aka-chan
**back** (n.) senaka
**bad** hukōna; warui
**badger** tanuki
**bad taste** (adj.) mazui
**bag** kaban
**bakery** pan'ya
**balcony** (in a theater) nikaiseki
**ballet** barē
**bamboo** take
**bandage** hōtai
**bank** ginkō; kishi
**bank account** ginkō-kōza
**bank deposit** yokin
**bar** bā; izakaya
**barber** tokoya
**bargain** bāgen
**baseball** yakyū

**basketball** basukettobōru
**bathroom** basu-rūmu
**be (to)** aru
**bear** kuma
**beautiful** kirei; utsukushii; subarashii
**beauty parlor** biyōin
**become** naru
**bedroom** shinshitsu
**beef** gyūniku
**beer** biiru
**before** mae
**before noon** gozen
**before yesterday** issakujitsu; ototoi
**behind** ushiro
**bell** shōrō
**belly** hara
**between** aida
**Bible** baiburu; seisho
**bicycle** jitensha
**big** dai; ookii
**biggest (the)** mottomo ōkii
**bill** (banknote) shihei
**bill of services** kanjōgaki
**biology** seibutsugaku
**bird** tori
**birthday** tanjōbi
**bitter** nigai
**black** kuroi
**black tea** kōcha
**bladder** bōkō
**blood** chi
**blood transfusion** yuketsu

**blow** (n.) dabokushō

**blue** aoi

**body** jintai; karada

**bone** hone

**book exhibition** shosekiten

**book** hon

**bookstore** shoten; hon'ya

**boring** tsumaranai

**bouillon** konsome

**boxing** bokusingu

**branch** (of office) shiten

**branch** eda

**bread** pan

**break (to)** yaburu; kowasu, kowareru

**breast** mune

**bridge** hashi

**brother(s)** kyodai

**brown** chairo

**brush** (n.) hude

**buckwheat noodle** soba

**buddha** hotoke-sama

**Buddhist priest** o-bōzan

**Buddhist temple** o-tera

**build (to)** tateru

**building number** banchi

**building** tatemono

**bus** basu

**bus stop** teiryūjo

**busy (to be)** husagaru

**busy** isogashii

**but** kedo; keredo; keredomo shikashi

**butter** batā

**buttocks** shiri
**buy (to)** kau

## C

**cabbage** kyabetsu
**calendar era** nengō
**camcorder** kamukōdā
**camera** kamera
**cameraman** kameraman
**canned food** kanzume
**captain** kyapten; senchō
**car** kuruma
**carrot** ninjin
**cash** (n.) genkin
**cashier** rejii
**cat** neko
**cauliflower** karifurawā
**caviar** kyabia
**center** chūō
**centimeter** senchimētoru
**cerebral hemorrhage** nōikketsu
**certified letter** haitatsu-shōmei yūbin
**champagne** shampen
**championship** senshuken-taikai
**change** (money) (n.) o-tsuri
**chapter** shō
**cheap** yasui
**cheerful** tanoshii
**cheese** chiizu
**chemistry** kagaku
**cherry** sakura

**chess** chesu
**child/children** kodomo/kodomotachi
**children's apparel** kodomohuku
**chilly** usura samui
**choked (to be)** husagaru
**chopsticks** hashi
**chrysanthemum** kiku
**church** kyōkaidō
**cinema** eiga
**circle** hiroba
**citizen** kokumin
**city** machi
**classical Japanese poem** utai; waka; haiku
**classic literature** (art) koten
**classroom** kyoshitsu
**clear** hare
**climate** kikō
**close (to)** *doors* shimeru
**close** chikai
**closed** (stores, restaurants) heiten; junbichū
 (closed now but open later in the day)
**clothes** yōhuku; irui
**clothing store** yōhukuya
**cloud** kumo
**cloudy** kumori
**coca cola** koka-kōra
**coffee** kōhii
**cognac** kon'yakku
**coin(s)** kōka
**cold** tsumetai; (weather) samui
**college** daigaku
**college graduate** gakushi

**color** iro
**come** (*1st person*) mairu; kuru
**comedy** kigeki
**comics** manga
**common** hutsū
**communication** tsūshin
**company** kaisha
**compassion** dōjō
**complete** shimau
**complete works** (books) sakuhinshū
**composer** sakkyokuka
**compulsory** hisshū; hissu
**computer** kompyūtā
**computer science** kompyūtā saiennsu
**conductor** (train) shashō
**conductor** (music) shikisha
**conference** kaigi
**congress** taikai
**connection** renraku, kone
**consolation** dōjō
**consulate** ryōjikan
**consultation** sōdan
**contact (to)** renraku-suru
**contacts** renraku, kone
**contemporary** gendai
**contents** mokuji
**contraceptive pills** piru
**cool** (good) kakkoii
**cool** suzushii
**correct** (adj.) kekkō
**correct (to)** naosu
**counter** uriba
**course** (discipline) kamoku

**cover** (book) hyōshi
**coward** okubyō-mono (n.)
**crab** kani
**cross** (a street) wataru (v.)
**cucumber** kyūri
**cultural exchange** bunka-kōryu
**culture** bunka
**cute** kawaii
**cuttlefish** ika


# D

**dance** odori (n.)
**danger** kiken
**data** jōhō
**daughter** musume
**day** (24 hours) nichi
**day** (as opposed to night) hiru
**day after tomorrow** asatte
**days of the week** yōbi
**December** jūnigatsu
**deep** hukai (adj.)
**delegation** daihyōdan
**delicious** (m.) umai; oishii
**dentist** shika-i
**department store** depāto
**departure** shuppatsu
**despair** yake
**dew** tsuyu
**diabetes** tōnyōbyō
**dictionary** jiten; jisho
**difficult** muzukashii

**dining room** shokudō
**director** (movie) kantoku
**disaster** sainan
**disco** disuko
**disgusting** iyani
**disturb** jamasuru (v.)
**divorce (to)** rikon-suru
**divorce** rikon
**do** (*only the 1st person*) itashu (very polite way)
**doctor** (Ph.D.) hakase; (M.D.) isha; (form of
    address) sensei
**dog** inu
**dramatist** gekisakka
**dream** yume
**dress** doresu
**drink (to)** nomu
**drink(s)** nomimono
**driver** untenshu
**drugstore** kusuriya
**drunkenness** meitei
**dry cleaning** dorai kuriiningu
**during** aida
**Dutch** Oranda
**dysentery** sekiri


## E

**early** hayai
**earthquake** jishin
**eat (to)** taberu
**education** (educational history) gakureki
**educational materials** kyōzai

**eel** unagi

**egg** tamago

**eight** hachi; yattsu

**eighth** dai-hachi-no

**eighty** hachijū

**elbow** hiji

**electric appliances store** denkiya

**electricity** denki

**elevator** erebētā

**eleventh** dai-jū ichi-no

**e-mail** ii-meiru

**embassy** taishikan

**emergency** hijyōji

**emperor** (Japanese) tennō

**encyclopedia** hyakka-jiten

**English** (person) Igirisu-jin; (adj.) Igirisu-no

**English-Japanese** Eiwa

**enjoy** tanoshimu

**enough (to be)** tariru

**enough** (no thank you) kekko; jūbun

**enter** (university) nyūgaku-suru

**entrance** iriguchi; (educational institution) nyūgaku

**entrance fee** nyūjōryō

**envelope** hūtō

**epicenter** shingenchi

**escalator** esukarētā

**evening** yūgata

**exam** shiken

**examination** (medical) shinsatsu

**exchange (to)** torikaeru

**excuse me** sumimasen

**exhibition** tenrankai

**exit** deguchi
**expensive** takai
**experience difficulties** komaru
**explain** setsumei-suru
**explanation** setsumei
**express** (train) kyūkō
**eye** me

# F

**face** kao
**factory** kōjō
**faculty** (division) gakubu
**fail** (general) shippaisuru; (an exam) shiken-ni
    ochiru
**fairy tale** otogi-banashi
**family** kazoku
**famous** yūmei-na
**fan** fan
**far** tooi
**fare adjustment machine** seisanki
**father** otō-san; chichi; chichioya
**fax** fakkusu
**fearful** kowai
**February** nigatsu
**field** nohara
**fifth** dai-go-no
**fifty** goju
**film** firumu
**finger** yubi
**finish** (n.) kesshōten; (v.) shimau, owaru
**firm** (company) kaisha

**first** (ordinal number) dai-ichi-no; (adj.) ichiban
**first-class car in a train** guriin-sha ("green car")
**fish** sakana
**five** go; itsutsu
**flood** kōzui
**flounder** hirame
**flower** hana
**fog** kiri
**folk** mingei; hitobito; kazoku
**follow** shitagau
**food** tabemono
**fool** (n.) baka
**foolish** baka-na; bakabakashii
**foolishness** bakabashisa
**foot** (body member) ashi; (measure) fiito
**football** (soccer) sakkā
**forecast** yohō
**forehead** hitai
**foreigner** gaijin; gaikokujin
**forest** mori
**foreword** jobun
**fork** fōku
**forty** yonjū
**four** yotsu
**fourth** dai-yon-no
**fox** kitsune
**France** Furansu
**free** (no charge) muryo; tada
**free choice** jijū-sentaku
**freedom** jiyū
**Friday** kin'yōbi
**frog** kaeru
**frost** shimo

**fruit** kudamono
**full** (adj.) ippai; (v.) ippai-ni-naru; fusagaru
**furniture** kagu


## G

**gallon** garon
**garlic** ninniku
**gastritis** i-kataru
**genitals** seishokuki
**geography** chirigaku
**geometry** kikagaku
**Germany** Doitsu
**get aboard** noru; jōsha-suru
**get drunk** you
**get off** (to) gesha-suru; oriru
**ginger** shōga
**given name** namae
**gizzard shad** kohada
**glad** ureshii
**glass** (drinking) koppu; (material) garasu
**glasses** megane
**gloomy** inkina
**glue** nori
**go** (to) yuku; iku
**go for it!** gambatte!
**good** ii; yoi; yoroshii; kekko
**good-bye** sayōnara
**Gospel** hukuinsho
**graduation** sotsugyō
**gram** guramu
**grandchild** mago

**granddaughter** magomusume
**grandma** o-bā-san; sobo
**grandpa** o-jii-san; sohu
**grandson** mago-musuku
**grape** budō
**Great Britain** Eikoku; Igirisu
**great** taihen; sugoi
**green** midori
**greengrocer** (fruit vendor) kudamonoya
**grocery** shokuryohin'ya
**guest** kyaku; raihin
**guest room** kyakuma
**guidebook** annaisho; gaidobukku
**guilt** tsumi
**guitar** gitā
**gum** haguki
**gymnastics** taisō


# H

**hair** kami
**half** hanbun
**ham** hamu
**hamburger** (with meat) hambāgu ; (with bread)
  hambāgā
**hand** te
**hangover** hutsuka yoi
**harsh** kibishii
**haze** kasumi
**he** (that person) kare
**head** atama
**heal** (v.) iyasu
**healing** (medical treatment) chiryō

**health** kenkō
**hear** kiku
**heart** (mental) kokoro; (organ) shinzō
**heart failure** shinzōbyō
**hero** eiyū
**herring** nishin
**higher education** kōtō kyōiku
**historian** rekishika
**history** rekishi
**Holland** Oranda
**homework** shukudai
**honeymoon** hanemūn; shinkon
**horseradish** wasabi (green); daikon (white)
**hospital** byōin
**host** (n.) shōtaigawa
**hot** atsui
**hotel** (Japanese-style) ryokan; (Western-style) hoteru
**hour** (period) jiikan; (time) ji
**house** ie
**housewife** shufu
**humidity** shitsudo
**humor** yūmoa
**hundred** hyaku
**hundred thousand** jūman
**hurricane** bōhu; taihū
**husband** (*general term*) otto; (*of the 1^st person*)
  shujin


**I**

**I** watakushi; watashi; atashi; boku (m.)
**ice** kōri

**iced tea** aisu tii
**idle chat** mandan
**illness** byōki
**image** imēji; zō; katachi
**importance** taisetsu
**impossible** muri
**indeed** naruhodo
**independence** dokuritsu
**infectious disease** densenbyō
**influenza** ryūkan
**information** jōhō
**information desk** annaijo; uketsuke
**in front of** mae-no; saki-no
**injection** chūsha
**injured (to be)** kega-wo suru
**innocent** mujitsu
**inscription** hibun
**institute** (educational institution) gakuin; kenkyūjo
**instruction** setsumei; shiji
**instrument** (music) gakki
**intention** tsumori; ito
**interest** kyōmi; rigai
**intermission** (theater) makuai ("between the stages"); (general) kyūkei
**internal medicine** naika
**interpretation** (translation) tsūyaku
**intersection** kōsaten
**invoice** (n.) seikyū-sho
**iris** ayame
**island** shima
**Israel** Isuraeru
**Israeli** Isuraeru-jin
**Italy** Itaria

**itchy (to be)** kayui
**ivory** zōge

## J

**jacket** uwagi
**January** ichigatsu
**Japanese clothing** wa huku; kimono
**Japanese socks** tabi
**Japanese style** washiki
**jazz** jazu
**jeans** jiinzu
**job** shigoto; tsutome
**jogging** jogingu
**journal** zasshi
**jovial** tanoshii
**judo** jūdō
**juice** jūsu
**July** shichigatsu
**jump (to)** tobikomu
**June** rokugatsu

## K

**karate** karate
**key** kagi
**kidney** jinzō
**kilogram** kiroguramu
**kilometer** kiro; kiromētoru
**kiosk** baiten; kiosuku
**kiss (to)** kisu

**kitchen** daidokoro; kicchin
**knee** hiza
**knife** naifu
**know** shiru


# L

**laboratory** jikkenshitsu
**ladies' apparel** fujinfuku
**lake** mizūmi
**lamb** yōniku
**lamp** dento
**landscape** sansui; keshishi
**laptop computer** rapputoppu-compyūtā
**large** dai; okii
**last month** sengetsu
**last week** senshū
**last year** kyonen
**late** osoi (adj.)
**laundry** sentaku; randorii; kuriiningu
**law** hōritsu
**law school** hōgakubu
**lecture** (general) jugyō; (college) kōgi
**lecture hall** kōdō
**left** hidari
**leg** ashi
**leisure** hima
**lemon** remon
**lesson** jugyō
**let (to)** yurusu
**letter** tegami
**letter paper** binsen

**library card** etsuran-ken
**library** toshokan; (home) zōsho
**like (to)** suki
**lilac** murasaki
**line** gyō; sen; retsu
**linguistics** gengogaku
**lip** kuchibiru
**liquor store** sakaya
**listen (to)** (v.) kiku
**liter** rittoru
**literature** bungaku
**live (to)** (dwell) zaijū
**liver** kanzō
**lobster** ise-ebi
**local (train)** hutsū
**look (to)** miru
**lose (to)** nakusu
**love (to)** ai-suru
**luggage** nimotsu
**lung** hai


## M

**mackerel** saba
**magazine** zasshi
**maid** mēdo-san
**mail** yūbin
**mailbox** (postal) posuto
**make a transfer** norikaeru
**man** hito; (m.) otoko
**manager** manējā
**manual** setsumeisho

**many** ōkuno; takusan
**map** chizu
**marathon** marason
**March** sangatsu
**marriage** kekkon
**marry** kekkon-suru
**match** shiai
**mathematician** sūgakusha
**mathematics** sūgaku
**matter** koto
**May** gogatsu
**meaning** imi; wake
**means of transportation** norimono; kōtsūshudan
**measure** saizu
**meat** niku
**medical science** igaku
**medication** toyāku
**meditation** zazen; meisō
**meet** au
**melon** meron
**memoirs** kaisōroku
**men's apparel** shishihuku
**men's suit** shinshiyō-sūtsu; sebiro
**message** kotozuke
**meter** mētoru
**midday** shōgo
**midnight** mayonaka
**mile** mairu
**milk** gyūnyū; miruku
**million** hyakuman
**ministry** shō
**minute** hun; pun
**mission** dendōkan

**missionary** senkyōshi

**mist** kiri

**monastery** (Buddhist) jiin; (Christian) shudōin

**Monday** getsuyōbi

**money** o-kane

**monk** (m.) shūdōso, o-bōsan; (f.) ama

**monkey** saru

**month** tsuki

**moon** tsuki

**more** motto

**morning** asa

**mother** hahaoya; o-kāsan; haha

**motherland** kokyō

**mountain** yama

**mouth** kuchi

**movie theater** eigakan

**Mr., Mrs.** (more polite form of *san*) sama

**much** (in negative context) amari; (in positive context) taihen

**muggy** mushiatsui

**muscle** kinniku

**museum** hakubutsukan

**mushrooms** ki-no ko

**music** ongaku


# N

**naive** ubu

**name** namae

**napkin** napukin

**nationality** kokuseki

**natural disaster** saigai

**near(by)** chikai; soba-no
**needle** hari
**nerve** shinkei
**nervous (to be)** aseru; shimpai-suru
**neuralgia** shinkeitsū
**newspaper** shimbun
**newsstand** shinbun-uriba
**next** tsugi
**next month** raigetsu
**next to** tonari; tsugi-no
**next week** raishu
**next year** rainen
**night** yoru
**nine** kokonotsu; kyū
**ninety** kyūjū
**ninth** dai-ku-no
**no** iie
**noisy** yakamashii; sōzōshii; urusai
**noodles** udon
**noon** shōgo
**nose** hana
**no smoking** kin'en
**notebook** nōto
**novel** shōsetsu
**November** jūichigatsu
**now** ima
**number** bango; sūji
**nurse** kangohu

# O

**occupation** shokugyō
**occupied (to be)** husagaru

**October** jūgatsu

**octopus** tako

**of course** mochiron

**office** (general) jimusho; (government) yakusho

**office window** madoguchi

**older brother** ani

**older sister** ane

**olive oil** oriibu oiru

**once** ichido

**one** hitotsu; ichi

**one day** ichinichi

**one hundred million** (*one* ichi) oku

**one month** (duration) ikkagetsukan

**one more** mō hitotsu

**one person** hitori

**one way** katamichi

**one week** isshūkan

**one year** ichinenkan

**onion** tamanegi

**on sale** sēru; ōuridashi

**open** (store or restaurant) eigyōchū

**open (to)** hiraku

**oracle** o-mikuji

**orange** (n.) orenji

**orchestra** gakudan; ōkesutora

**order slip** (in a library) seikyūhyō

**organ** (instrument) orugan

**original** (not translation) gensho

**orphan** minashigo; koji

**Orthodox Christian priest** shisai

**otolaryngology** jibiinkōka

**ounce** onsu

**out of order** (not working) kosho

**overcoat** obā(kōtō)

# P

**page** pēji
**painting** kaiga
**panoramic view** zenkei
**pants** zubon
**paper** kami
**parcel** kozutsumi
**parents** ryōshin
**park** kōen
**part** bun
**participate** (in a ceremony) sanretsu-suru
**pass an exam** shiken-ni gōkaku-suru
**path** michi
**pavilion** tenjikan
**peach** momo
**pear** nashi
**pediatrics** shōnika
**pen** pen
**pencil** enpitsu
**people** hitobito
**percent** pāsento
**performance** (drama) shibai
**permit (to)** yurusu
**persimmon** kaki
**pestering** naya masu; komaraseru
**pharmacy** kusuri'ya
**photography exhibit** shashinten
**photo shop** kamera'ya
**physician** isha
**physics** butsuri (gaku)
**piano** piano

**picture** e
**picture exhibition** kaigaten
**pig** buta
**pills** jōzai; (contraceptive) piru
**pilot** sōjū-shi
**pine tree** matsu
**pineapple** painappuru
**place** basho
**plan** an; chizu
**plant** kōjō
**plastic surgery** seikeigeka
**plate** sara
**platform** hōmu
**play** (n.) geki
**play (to)** (musical instruments) hiku; ensō-suru
**playwright** geki-sakka
**pleasant** tanoshii
**please** dōzo; kudasai
**pleurisy** rokumakuen
**plot** purotto; kuwadate
**plum** (fruit) sumomo
**plum tree** ume-no-ki
**pneumonia** haien
**poem** shi; tanka; waka; haiku
**poet** shijin
**poisoning** chūdoku
**policeman** keikan
**police post** kōban
**pond** ike
**popular** yumei-na
**population** jinkō
**pork** butaniku

**porter** akabō
**portrait** shōzō
**position** shokuseki
**postcard** hagaki
**post office** yūbinkyoku
**post office box** (P.O.B.) shishobako
**potato** poteto; jagaimo
**pound** pondo
**prawn** taisho-ebi
**prayer** inori
**preacher** dendōshi
**prescription** shohōsen
**presidium** gichōdan
**press center** puresu-sentā
**press conference** kisha-kaiken
**price** nedan; kakaku
**priest** (general) seishokusha; (Christian) bokushi;
    (Shinto) kannushi
**print** (engraving) hanga
**printed materials** insatsu-butsu
**probably** tabun
**profession** shokugyō
**professor** kyōju
**program** nittei; puroguramu
**programming** (computer) puroguraminngu
**project** an; purojecto
**prose** sambun
**proverb** kotowaza
**pub** pabu
**publishing house** shuppansha
**puzzled** (**to be**) komaru; nayamu

# Q

**quiet** shizuka-na

# R

**racing** kyōsō
**radish** akakabu
**rain** ame
**rain cloud** amagumo
**raincoat** renkōto
**ranger** shinrin-kanshinin
**rave** (n.) wameki: (v.) wameku
**raw fish** (dish) sashimi
**read (to)** yomu
**reading room** etsuran-shitsu
**really** hontō
**reason** (cause) wake; yue; riyū
**receipt** ryōshūsho
**receptionist** (front desk) furonto-san; uketsuke
**record** (memo, a note; sport) kiroku
**red (salmon) roe** ikura
**red** (adj.) akai; (n.) aha
**red wine** akabudōshu; akawain
**referee** referii
**refreshment** oyatsu; keishoku
**registered letter** kakitome-yūbin
**registration** tōroku
**regret** zannen; kyōshuku
**relative** shinseki; shinrui
**religion** shyūkyō

**renovation** teire; kaishū
**rent** yachin
**repair** (n.) shūri
**repair (to)** naosu
**repartee** mandan
**repertoire** repātorii
**required** hisshū
**reserved seat** zaseki shitei (train); yoyaku-seki
(restaurant)
**rest** (n.) yasumi
**rest (to)** yasumu
**restaurant car** shokudōsha
**return (to)** (v.int.) kaeru; (v.t.) kaesu
**rice** (raw) hakumai; (cooked) raisu; gohan
**rice with curry** karē-raisu
**right** migi
**risk** bōken
**risky** kikenna
**river** kawa
**road** michi; dōro
**robbery** dorobō
**rock climbing** tozan
**rock-n-roll** rokku-n-rōru
**roe** harago; tarako (cod roe)
**room** heya
**round trip** (ticket) ōhuku
**run (to)** hashiru
**rush hour** rasshu awā
**Russia** Roshia


S

**sad** kanashii
**sake** sake

**sale** oūridashi

**salesperson** ten'in

**salt** shio

**sample** mihon

**sandals** sandaru

**sandwich** sandoicchi

**sardine** iwashi

**Saturday** doyōbi

**sausage** sōsēji

**scallion** naganegi

**scallop** hotategai

**scene** (part of performance) bamen

**scholar** gakusha

**school** gakkō

**sclerosis** dōmyaku kōka

**season** kisetsu

**seat for the elderly and disabled** sirubā-siito ("silver seat")

**seat** seki

**second** (adj.) dai-ni-no

**second** (n.) byo

**second-hand store** chūkoya

**secretariat** jimukyoku

**sect** (religious) shūha

**see (to)** miru

**semester** gakki

**seminar** zemināru; semiā

**send** okuru

**sentence** bunshō

**September** kugatsu

**sermon** sekkyō

**service bill** kanjō-gaki
**service** (religious) reihaishiki
**set a record** (sport) kiroku-wo tsukuru
**seven** nana; nanatsu; shichi
**seventh** dai-shichi-no
**seventy** shichiju
**sex** sekkusu
**sexy** iroppoi *(slang)*
**shame** haji
**she** kanojo
**Shintoist shrine** jinja
**Shinto priest** kannushi
**shoes** kutsu
**shop** (n.) mise
**shopping mall** shoppingu-sentā
**shore** kishi
**short story** tampen-shosetsu
**shoulder** kata
**shout (to)** sakebu
**show (to)** miseru
**shrimp** (small) koebi
**side** (general) wakihara
**sightseeing** kembutsu; kankō
**silk** kinu; (100% silk) honken
**silver** gin
**sing** utau
**single** (not married) dokushin
**sister(s)** shimai
**sitting mat** zabuton
**six** muttsu; roku
**sixth** dai-roku-no
**sixty** rokujū

**skating** sukēto

**skillful** jōzu-na

**skin** (human) hihu; (fruit, animal) kawa

**skirt** sukāto

**sky** sora

**sleep (to)** nemuru

**sleeping car** shindaisha

**sleepy** nemui

**sleet** mizore

**slippers** surippa

**slow** nibui; osoi

**slowly** yukkuri

**small** chiisai

**smart** rikō-na

**snacks** oyatsu; sunakku

**snow** yuki

**society** shakai

**sociology** shakaigaku

**socks** sokkusu

**son** musuko

**song** uta

**soon** hayaku; sugu

**sorry** sumimasen

**sound** oto

**sour** suppai

**space** ma; aida

**speak** hanasu; iu; (at a conference, etc.) hatsugen-suru

**special delivery** (express mail) sokutatsu

**special express** (train) tokkyu

**special price** (sale) tokka

**specialty** senmon

**spicy** karai

**spirit** ki; tamashii; kokoro

**splendid** subarashii

**spoon** supūn

**sports** supōtsu

**sportsman** supōtsuman

**spring** haru

**square** (city) hiroba

**stage** (place of performance) butai

**stairs** kaidan

**star** hoshi

**start** sutāto; hajimari

**station** eki

**station officer** ekiin

**statue** (bronze) dōzō; (stone) seki-zō

**steak** sutēki

**stepchild** mamako

**stepfather** gihu

**stepmother** mamahaha; gibo

**stomach** i

**stomachache** i-tsū

**stop (to)** (v.t.) tomeru; tomaru (v.int.)

**storm** arashi

**straight** massugu

**strange** hushigina

**street corner** kado

**street crossing** ōdan-hodo

**street** tōri; dōro

**strong** tsuyoi; (drink) tsuyoi; (coffee, tea) koi

**study (to)** benkyō-suru; manabu

**study room** shosai

**stupid** baka-na

**subject of conversation** wadai

**subway** chikatetsu

**sugar** satō

**summer** natsu

**summer kimono** yukata

**sumo wrestling** sumō

**sun** hi; taiyō

**Sunday** nichiyōbi

**sunrise** hinode

**sunset** nichibotsu; hinoiri

**supermarket** sūpā (maketo)

**surely not** masaka

**surgery** shujutsu; (department) geka

**surname** miyoji; sei

**surprised (to be)** odoroku

**sushi bars** hushiya

**sweater** sētā

**sweet** amai

**swim (to)** oyogu

**swimming** suiei

**symphony orchestra** kōkyō-gakudan; ōkesutora

**symphony** simfonii

**symposium** simpoziumu

**symptoms** shōjō

**syringe** chūshyaki


# T


**table** tsukue; tēburu

**talk** (n.) hanashi

**tampon** tampakkusu

**tangerine** mikan

**tasteless** mazui

**tea** cha (o-cha)

**teacher** sensei

**team** chiimu

**telegram** dempō

**telephone** denwa

**telephone directory** denwachō

**television** terebi

**tell** iu; tsutaeru

**temperature** (general) ondo; (air) kion; (body) taion

**ten** jū; tō

**tender** (food) yawarakai; (emotional) yasashii

**tenth** dai-jū-no

**ten thousand** man

**terminal** (n.) eki; tāminaru

**terrible** hidoi; kibishii

**terrific** sugoi

**test** kensa

**textbook** kyōkasho

**thank you** arigatō

**that** (adj.) ano

**that** (n.) are

**thaw** (n.) yukidoke

**theater** (art) kōen; (drama) engeki

**theater** (building) gekijō

**theater** (troupe) gekidan

**theme** tēma

**they** (people) hitobito; (non-human) sorera

**thing** mono

**think** kangaeru; omou

**third** dai-san-no

**thirsty (to be)** nodo-ga kawaku

**thirty** sanjū

**this** (adj.) sono

**this** (adj.) (closer to speaker) kono

**this** (n.) sore

**this** (n.) (closer to speaker) kore

**this month** kongetsu

**this week** konshū

**this year** kotoshi

**thousand** sen

**three** mitsu; san

**Thursday** mokuyōbi

**ticket** kippu

**ticket box** kippu uriba

**till** made

**time** toki; jikan

**timetable** jikokuhyō

**tired (to be)** tsukareru

**title** (book) hyōdai

**to** made

**today** konnichi; kyo

**toilet** toire; o-tearai ("hand-washing place");
    keshōshitsu ("powder room"); semmenjo
    ("washroom")

**tomato** tomato

**tomorrow** ashita

**tongue** shita

**tooth/teeth** ha

**totally** sappari; mattaku; zenzen (negative)

**touch** sawaru

**town** machi

**town block** machi

**traditional** (folk) dentō-tekina

**traditional Japanese sandals** geta

**tragedy** higeki

**train** (n.) densha; kisha; ressha

**trainer** torēnā

**tram** romen-densha

**tranquilizer** chinseizai

**transfer** norikae

**translation** honyaku

**travel agency** ryokōsha

**traveler's check** toraberāzu chekku

**tree** ki

**Tuesday** kayōbi

**tuna** maguro

**turn (to)** (on road) magaru

**turnip** kabu

**twenty** nijū

**twilight** higure; tasogare

**two** hutatsu; ni

**typhoon** taihu


U


**uncle** oji

**underground walkway** chikadō

**underground shopping area** chikagai

**understand** wakaru

**underwear** shitagi

**unhappiness** huko
**university** daigaku
**urinary organs** hinyōki
**usual** hutsū


# V

**vegetables** yasai
**very** totemo
**very bad** hidoi
**very much** dōmo; mottomo
**viewing** kanran
**violent** hageshii
**violet** murasaki
**violin** baiorin
**visitor** hōmonsha
**vocal music** seigaku
**vodka** uokka
**voice** koe
**volcano** kazan
**vote (to)** tōhyō-suru


# W

**waist** uesuto
**wait (to)** matsu
**waiting hall** machiaishitsu
**walk (to)** aruku
**wallet** saihu
**warm** atatakai
**watch** tokei

**water** mizu

**watermelon** suika

**water temperature** suion

**way** michi; (means) hōhō

**we** watakushitachi; wareware

**weak** (physically) yowai; (coffee, tea) usui

**weather** tenki

**wedding ceremony** kekkon-shiki

**Wednesday** suiyōbi

**weight** omosa

**Western clothing** yōhuku

**Western style** yōshiki

**wet** nureta; shimetta

**what** nani

**when** itsu

**which** dore; dono, dochira

**white** shiroi

**white wine** shirobudōshu; shiro-wain

**who** dare; donata

**wife** (*general term*) tsuma; (*of the 1st person—* "*my*") kanai; (*of the 2nd and 3rd person*) okusan

**wind** kaze

**wine** budō-shu; wain

**winter** huyu

**with all** (my, your) isshōkemmei

**woman** hujin; onna; joei

**work (to)** hataraku; shigoto-wo suru

**worker** rōdōsha

**wound** husho; kizu

**wrap up** (an object) tsutsumu; (a topic) matomeru

**wrestling** resuringu

**write** kaku

**writer** sakka
**wrong (to be)** chigau; machigau; (person)
machigaeru


# X

**X ray** rentogen


# Y

**year** toshi
**yearbook** nenkan
**yellow** kiiro
**yen** en
**yes** ee; hai
**yesterday** kinō
**you** (informal) kimi; (sg.) anata; (pl.) anatagata
**young** wakai
**younger brother** otōto
**younger sister** imōto


# Z

**zero** rei; zero
**zoologist** dōbutsu-gakusha

## JAPANESE PHRASEBOOK

*For usage of the backslash ( / / / ), see Introduction.

## 1. FORMS OF ADDRESS, GREETINGS, INTRODUCTIONS, AND POLITENESS

**Forms of Address**

When addressing an unknown person, one should start with an apology:

Excuse me, but... **(Chotto) sumimasen ga...**
I beg your pardon... **(Chotto) shitsurei desu ga...**
Sorry for being late. **(Sumimasen.) Taihen
    o-matase itashimashita.**
Sorry for disturbing you. **O-isogashii tokoro-wo
    ojama-shite sumimasen.**

After the name of the person one should add the polite suffix *-san* or *-sensei*: **Yamamoto-san** or **Yamamoto-sensei**. The latter is usually used when addressing teachers and professors. Literally, it means "born before." When addressing friends or minors, it is appropriate to say *-kun*, but only in informal situations: **Yōkichi-kun** or **Yamada-kun**. When addressing small children, the suffix *-chan* is added to the name: **Yukiko-chan**.

**Greetings**

Hello! **Konnichi-wa!** (the generic greeting which
    can be used in formal situations during the day)

# FORMS OF ADDRESS

Good morning! **Ohayō gozaimasu!**

Good evening! **Komban-wa!**

Welcome! **Yōkoso oide kudasaimashita!; Yoku irasshaimashita!**

Come in, please. **Dōzo o-hairi kudasai.**

This way, please. **Kochira-e dōzo.**

How are you? **O-genki desu ka?**

---

### Young People's Language

*What's up? **Nanka kawatta-koto atta?***

*Nothing special. **Betsu-ni.***

*How are you? **Genki?***

*I'm fine. (feminine tone) **Genki-yo!***

*Is Setsuko okay? **Setsuko wa genki?***

---

## Congratulations and Toasts

Congratulations! **Omedetō gozaimasu!**

Happy birthday! **O-tanjōbi omedetō!**

Happy New Year! **Shinnen omedetō gozaimasu!**

I wish you happiness! **Go-kōhuku-wo o-inori itashimasu!**

**Kampai!** (*the shortest form of a toast*)

To our friendship! **Watakushitachi-no yūjō-no tame-ni kampai shimashō!**

To your health! **Anata-no go-kenkō-wo iwai kampai shimashō!**

## Introductions

Let me introduce myself. I'm John Smith.
**Watakushi-wa Sumisu desu. Dozō yoroshiku.**

May I know your name, please? **O-namae-wa nanto osshaimasu ka?**

Nice to meet you. **Hajimete o-me-ni kakarimasu.**

I heard so much about you. **O-namae-wa kanegane ukagatte imashita.**

**Introduce** me to Mr. Yamada, please. **Yamada-san-ni** *goshōkai*(-shite) **itadakemasen ka?**

Let me introduce you, Mr. Clinton. **Kurinton-san-wo goshōkai itashimasu.**

I came to Japan as a tourist. **Watakushi-wa kankō kyaku toshite Nihon-e mairimashita.**

Where are you **from**? **Anata-wa** *doko kara* **irasshaimashita ka?**

I am in Japan for the first time. **Watakushi-wa Nihon-wa hajimete desu.**

We came from America. **Watakushitachi-wa Amerika kara /kimashita/ mairimashita.**

**Model Introductory Dialogues**

Excuse me, are you Mr. Kuroda? **Shitsurei desu ga, Kuroda-san desu ka?**

Yes, I'm Kuroda. **Hai, Kuroda desu keredomo.**

Hello! I'm John Smith. Nice to meet you. **Konnichi-wa. Watakushi-wa Sumisu desu. Hajimemashite.**

Nice meeting you. **Hajimete o-me-ni kakarimasu.**

Good morning! **O-hayō gozaimasu.**

Though Japanese people do not say "How are you?" often, you could say:

How are you? **Genki desu ka?**

Hello! I'm fine *(lit. "healthy")*. You? **O-hai. Genki desu yo. Anata-wa?**

I'm fine. Thank you. **Genki desu.**

### Weather

Traditionally *all* Japanese conversations begin with remarks about the weather. See also chapter 21 (Weather and Climate).

It's such **wonderful weather** today! **Kyōwa *ii o-tenki* desu ne!**

Today is very... **Kyowa... desu.**

| | |
|---|---|
| ...hot. | **...atsui...** |
| ...muggy. | **...mushiatsui...** |
| ...warm. | **...atatakai desu...** |
| ...cold. | **...samui...** |
| ...cool. | **...suzushii...** |

Today is **horrible** weather. **Kyo-wa *iyana* tenki desu.**

It's a very **hot** summer this year, isn't it? **Kotoshi-no natsu-wa taihen *atsui* desu ne?**

## 2. CONVERSATION

During conversation with the Japanese, it is important to show your reaction to your interlocutor from time to time. The party who listens is expected to indicate that he/she is listening, understands, agrees, hesitates, etc. These short expressions are very important. The best word for many purposes is **hai** *("yes" or just "understand")*.
Other expressions:

Oh, really? **Sō desu ka?**
Yes, I follow you. **Sō desu ne.**
I see. **Naruhodo.**

---

**Young People's Language**
*Really?* **Honto?**
*No kidding?* **Masaka!**
*Is that so? (feminine tone)* **Sō-nano?**
*Did you? Do you?* **Sō-nano?**
*How come?* **Dō-shite?**
*Why?* **Nande?**
*Maybe.* **Tabun.**

---

**Agreement**

Yes, that's right. **Ee, so desu.**
Oh, yes. **So so so.** *(mostly in women's speech)*
For sure! **Mochiron desu!**
Yes, indeed! **Mattaku desu ne/Sonotōri desu!**
I think so, too. **Watakushi-mo so omoimasu.**

Naturally! **Mochirou/Tōzen!**
No objections. **Iron arimasen.**
All right. **Kekko desu.**

---
**Young People's Language**

*That's right. (men speaking)* **So-dane.**
*I swear! (feminine tone)* **Zettai-yo!**
*Response to a statement made by another*
*   person:* **Mattaku sonotōri.**

---

The following phrases can be used to express agreement at the end of a conversation:

Yes. **Hai.**
Yes, I'll do that. **Hai, sō shimasu.**
O.K. let's do it that way. **Hai, sō shimashō.**
Okay, do this. **Dewa so shite moraimashō.**
I'll definitely do this. **Kanarazu sō shimasho.**
O.K., I agree. *(to a junior person)* **Hai, yoroshii desu.**
I'll do as you said. **O-hanashi-no toori-ni**
   **itashimasu.**
O.K. Agreed! **Sansei desu.**
Promise! **Dewa, yakusoku-shimashita.**
Well, I'll think about it. **Dewa kentō shimashō.**
I'll try to do it. **Kore-wo yatte mimasu.**
I'll do the best I can. **Isshōkenmei yatte mimasu.**

---
**Young People's Language**

*Leave it up to me!* **Makashite oke!**
*Sure!* **Mochirou!**
*Deal!* **Kimari!**

---

**Comprehension**

What? **Nan desu tte?** *(this implies "I don't agree with you.")*

What do you mean? **To iimasu to?**

What does it mean? **Sore-wa dōyū koto desu ka?**

I cannot understand you. **Domo kikitoremasen.**

Speak more **slowly**, please. **Mo sukoshi** *yukkuri* **itte kudasai.**

Sorry, would you please say it **again. Sumimasen ga,** *mō ichido* **itte kudasai.**

---

**Young People's Language**

*What do you mean?* **Do-iu imi?**

*What?* **Nani?**

---

**Hesitation, Objection and Disagreement**

Is it so? Well, I don't know. **Sō desu ka nē?**

Really? **Sō desu ka?**

Oh, no, it cannot be so. **Masaka!**

You are kidding. **Go-jodan deshō/Masaka!** *(the latter used among businesspeople)*

This is strange. **Sore-wa /myo/hen desu.**

Yes, but... **Shikashi, desu ne...**

No, I disagree. **Iya, husansei desu.**

No, I can't. **(Watakushi-wa) dekimasen.**

No. **Iie.**

No way. **Tondemonai.**

Sorry, but I'm **busy. Zannen desu ga,** **(watakushi-wa)** *isogashikute* **dame desu.**

I'm afraid you made a mistake. **Anata-ga machigatte iru to omoimasu.**

# CONVERSATION

> **Young People's Language**
> *How come?* **Do-shite?**
> *Are you serious?* **Honki?**
> *Are you sure?* **Honto-ni?**
> *I doubt it.* **Masaka.**
> *I don't think so.* **So omowanai.**

## Interruption

Well, but… **Shikashi desu ne.**

It's all fine **but**… **Sore-wa kekko desu,** *ga…*

Sorry for interrupting (you). **O-hanashi-chu shitsurei desu ga.**

I didn't mean that. **Sonna tsumori de wa nai no desu.**

No. So what? **Iie. Sorede?**

Don't **interrupt** me, please. **Hanashi-no koshi-wo *oranaide* kudasai.**

Listen to me *(lit.: "a bit more")*, please. **Ma, mō sukoshi kiite kudasai.**

Let me finish. **Shimai-made shaberasete kudasai/Owari-made hanasasete kudasai.**

Let's change the subject. **Wadai-wo/Hanashi-wo kaemashō.**

> **Young People's Language**
> *Why not?* **Nande dame-nano?**

## Gratitude

Thank you. *(mostly neutral)* **Arigato gozaimasu.**

Thank you, I'm fine. **O-kage-sama-de.** *(lit.: "I'm well thanks to your prayers.")*

Thank you *(when offered something, like a meal or a present)*. **Itadakimasu.** *("I'll respectfully take (it).")*

Thank you and good-bye. **O-tsukare-sama.** *(at the end of a workday, etc.)*

*Answer:* Don't mention it. **Dōitashimashite.**

**Saying Good-bye**

Well, it's high time to go. **Soro soro o-itoma shinakute-wa...**

Good-bye. *(most common form)* **Sayōnara.**

There are various forms of "good-bye" said in specific situations:

*(to relatives leaving home for sometime)* **Itterasshai.**
*(the departing person to relatives staying home)* **Itte mairimasu.**
*(leaving work or leaving a party)* **Shitsurei shimasu.** ("Excuse me for leaving before you.")
*(to the host after a meal)* **Go-chisō-sama deshita.**
*(when someone leaving wishes to express gratitude)* **Go-kurō-sama deshita/O-tsukare-san; /O-sewa-sama.**
*(when parting for a long time)* **Dōzo o-tassha-de.**
*(to sick patients)* **Dewa o-daiji-ni** *("Be well")*.
Bon voyage. **Dozo go-buji-de.**
Take care of your health. **O-karada-wo taisetsu-ni.**

More casual ways to say good-bye, like "bye" or "so long":

**Dewa shitsurei.**

**O-saki-ni.**

**Dewa shikkei** (*used mainly in the business world*).

---

**Young People's Language**

*See you tomorrow.* **Ashita mata ne.**

*See you soon.* **Mata ne (na); Ja ne (na).**

The end particle *-ne* is used by girls and also by boys speaking to girls. **Na** is used only by boys.

---

## 3. REQUESTS

### Simple Requests

The easiest way to ask for something is to point to the object you want and say *kore-wo* ("this," if it is closer to you than to the other person) or *sore-wo* ("that," if it's closer to another person) and add one of the following phrases:

Give me this thing (book, water), please. **Kore-wo (hon-wo, mizu-wo) kudasai.**

Bring me that thing (beer), please. **Sore-wo (biru-wo) motte kite kudasai.**

**Bring** us two cups of tea, please. **(Sumimasen ga), kōcha-wo futatsu *motte kite* kudasai.**

Show me this (kimono), please. **Kore-wo (kimono-wo) misete kudasai.**

### Asking for Something

Explain it to me, please. **Setsumei shite kudasai.**

Translate, please. **Yakushite kudasai.**

Tell me, please. **Osshatte kudasai.**

Walk me to the door, please. **Doa made annai-shite kudasai.**

May I come in? **Gomen kudasai/Haittemo iidesuka?**

May I smoke here? **Tabako-wo sutteno mo kamaimasen ka?**

Faster, please. **(Dōzo) isoide kudasai.**

### More Sophisticated Forms of Request

If you want to be polite, always begin a request with an apology: "Excuse me,…"– *sumimasen ga*…, or the introductory phrase: "I want to ask you something"—**O-negai-ga aru no desu ga.** The phrase should be completed by *kudasai*—"please."

Would you please **explain** this to me? **Kore-wo** *setsumei*-**shite kudasaimasen ka**?

After requesting something, pause and listen to the reaction of your interlocutor.

Your request might be answered by one of the following:

### Consent

Sure. **Mochiron.**
Okay. **Ii desho.**
Ready to serve you. **Nannarito dozo.**
I'm listening to you. **O-ukagai-shimashō.**
I'm delighted (*to do something for you*).
    **Yorokonde shimashō.**

### Disagreement

Sorry, I **can't** help. **Zannen desu ga,** *dekimasen.*
Don't ask me, I **cannot** do that. **O-tanomi-ni nattemo,** *muda/muri* **desu.**
Well, I'd rather not do that ("it's a little **difficult**").
    **Saa, sore-wa chotto** *komarimasu* **ne.**

You'd better ask Mr. Matsumoto. **Matsumoto-san-ni tanonde goran-nasai.**

**Need/Wish**

There are different ways to express that you need or want something. Unfortunately, the most commonly used way is convenient only for persons with a certain understanding of Japanese. A wish to do something is expressed with the help of the suffix *-tai* followed by the verbal form *desu*. They follow the main verb, which ends with a letter *-i*. In informal situations, you may drop *desu*.

I **want to go** to the movies. **Eigakan-e *ikitai* desu.**
I'd **like to meet** Mr. Sasaki. **Sasaki-san-ni *oai-shitaino* desuga/Sasaki-san ni o-*me-ni* kakaritai no desu ga.**

The negative form is ***taku arimasen***:

I **don't want** to go there. **Asoko-e *ikitaku arimasen.***

A wish/need for something (noun) is expressed by the particle *hoshii* after the object:

I **need** (am looking for) **a book** with stories for children. **Kodomo-no o-hanashi-no *hon-ga hoshii* no desu ga.**
I **want** (to buy) some Japanese **teacups.** (**Nihon-no**) *chawan-ga hoshii* **no desu ga.**

A need to do something is formed by the word *hitsuyo* ("necessity") + *desu*:

I need (to do, to buy, to have) this. **Kore-wa hitsuyo desu.**

An obligation or necessity is expressed with *nakereba naranai* (more polite form: *nakereba narimasen*), which is used with verbs ending with *-a*:

I have to work. **Watakushi-wa shigoto-wo shinakereba naranai.**

(I, you, he/she, we) **need(s) to write** a letter. **Tegami-wo *kakanakereba narimasen*.**

The simplest way to express your intention is to use the form *tsumori* ("plan") + *desu* after the verb in its infinitive form (ending with -*u*).

We are going to return to our country tomorrow. **Ashita (watakushitashi-wa) kikoku-suru tsumori desu.**

I also plan to take part in it. **Watakushi-mo sanka-suru tsumori desu.**

## 4. EXPRESSION OF EMOTIONS

The following expressions might be used with all topics from the thematic part of this book (chapters 6–25).

**Joy, Satisfaction**

How nice that it turned out this way. **Sore-wa yokatta desu ne.**
How wonderful! **Sore-wa arigatai!**
Oh, I'm (you're, he/she is) lucky. **Aa, un-ga ii desu ne.**
Pleased to hear it. **Sore-wo ukagatte ureshii desu.**
Splendid! **Subarashii desu ne.**

**Regret**

It's such a pity! **Zannen desu ne!**
Oh, such a terrible thing! **Nante hukōna koto desho!**
I share your sorrow. **Go-dōjō mōshiagemasu**.
*(Expressing surprise, for example about an unexpected gift).* **Sorewa, sorewa!**
I'm very sorry. **O-kinodoku desu.**

**Difficulties/Problems**

I'm in trouble. **Komatta koto-ni narimashita.**
What can I do? **Dōshitara iideshō.**
What's the matter? **Dōshimashita ka?**

**Anxiety, Fear**

I feel uneasy (about this matter). **(Kono koto-ga)
   kigakari desu.**
Did I offend you? **Nanika o-ki-ni sawarimashita ka?**
I am afraid. **(Watakushi-wa) shimpai desu.**

**Uncertainty, Hesitations**

Well, let me think... **Eetoo...** (*very popular
   expression at the beginning of a sentence*)
Well, what can I say... **So desu ne...**
It depends. **Baai ni yori masuga...**

---

**Young People's Language**
*I doubt it. **Masaka.***
*I can't say for sure. **Tashika ja nai.***

---

**Disagreement, Anger**

Of course, not! **Tondemonai!**
What rubbish! **Nanda bakana!**
Shame on you! **Kono hajisarashime-ga!**
Isn't it a shame! **Nantoyū hajisarashi!**
That's impossible! **Muri-desu!**

---

**Young People's Language**
*Leave me alone! **Hitori-ni shite!**/**Hottoite** (f.)*
*It's none of your business! **Yokeina osewa!***
*No way! **Tondemonai/Jō-danja nai.***

---

## 5. LANGUAGE

Do you speak **English**? (**Anata-wa**) *eigo*-wo
  **hanashimasu ka?**

Let's speak in English. **Eigo-de hanashimashō
  ka?**

I don't speak Japanese. **Watakushi-wa nihongo-
  wo hanashimasen.**

I understand. **Wakarimashita.**

I don't understand. **Wakarimasen.**

What **languages** do you speak? (**Anata-wa**)
  **donna** *gaikoku go*-wo **hanashimasu ka?**

I know… **Watakushi-wa … -ga dekimasu.**

| …English. | **…eigo…** |
| …French. | **…furansugo…** |
| …German. | **…doitsugo…** |
| …Russian. | **…rossiago…** |

I know a **little** Japanese. (**Watakushi-wa**) *sukoshi*
  **nihongo-ga dekimasu.**

I wish to learn Japanese. (**Watakushi-wa**)
  **nihongo-wo benkyō shitai desu.**

I can **understand** you. (**Watakushi-wa**) **anata-no
  ossharu koto-ga** *wakarimasu*.

Understood. **Wakatta.**

I don't understand you. **Chotto wakarimasen.**

Speak more **slowly,** please. **Mōsukoshi,** *yukkuri*
  **hanasite kudasai.**

**Repeat**, please. *Mo ichi do onegaishimasu.*

What does this word (character) **mean**? **Kono
  kotoba (kono ji)-wa** *dōyū imi* **desu ka?**

**How** do I **say** this in Japanese? **Kore-wa
  nihongo-de** *nanto iimasu* **ka?**

Please **translate** this. *Tsūyaku*-ga **hitsuyō desu.**

Would you please call an interpreter? (**Dozo**)
  **tsūyaku-wo yonde kudasai.**

**Translate** what he said, please. **Anohito-no iu
  koto-wo tsuyaku-shite kudasai.**

Please translate what is **written** here. **Koko-ni
  nanto** *kaite* **aru ka, yakushite kudasai.**

We understand each other without translation.
  **Watakushitachi-wa tsuyaku-ga nakute mo
  wakarimasu.**

## 6. ASKING FOR DIRECTIONS

I'm a foreigner and don't know the city.
**Watakushi-wa gaikokujin-de kono machi-wo shirimasen.**

What's the name of this square (street)? **Kore-wa nan toyū hiroba (toori) desu ka?**

Where does this street lead? **Kono toori-wa doko-e iku no desu ka?**

What's the name of this area? **Kono atari-wa nanto iimasu ka?**

Would you please tell me how to get to (Ginza)? **(Ginza)-made dō yatte ikeba ii deshō ka?**

Would you explain the way to go to... **...-e iku michi-wo oshiete kudasai.**

Which bus should I take to... **...-e yuku no-wa dono basu desu ka?**

How can I get to the center of the city? **Machi-no chūō e wa dō ikeba ii desu ka?**

In what district are the biggest stores? **Ichiban ookii shōten-gai-wa doko desu ka?**

I am **lost.** **(Watakushi-wa)** *michi-ni /mayotte* **shimaimashita/mayoimashita.**

Where am I? **Koko-wa doko desu ka?**

Where are we now on this **map**? **Koko-wa kono** *chizu*-**de doko desu ka?**

Could you **draw** me a map, please? **Chizu-wo** *kaite* **kudasai.**

Where is the U.S. Consulate? **Amerika ryōjikan-wa doko desu ka?**

Is there a **police** station nearby? **Kono chikaku-ni** *kōban*-**wa arimas ka?**

Is it **far?** **Koko-kara** *tooi* **desu ka?**

# ASKING FOR DIRECTIONS

Is it **near**? *Chikaku* **desu ka?**

Yes, it's pretty far. **Ee, kanari tooi desu.**

No, it's nearby. **Iie, chikai desu.**

Can I walk there? **Aruite ikemasu ka?**

Turn to the left (right) at the **next corner**. *Tsugi-no kado*-**wo hidari (migi)-ni magarinasai.**

Explain it **again**, please. *Mō ichido* **setsumeishite kudasai.**

You are going in the wrong direction. **Michi-ga chigatte imasu.**

I'll **wait** for you here. **Koko-de** *matte* **imasu.**

## Restrooms (Toire)

Many foreign visitors are pleasantly surprised about the number, tidiness and convenience of public restrooms in Japan. They can be found in many places: in parks, playgrounds, subway and railway stations, stores, etc. Most facilities have Japanese-style toilets (the "non-touch" system: just a hole in the floor). In hotels and department stores, there are also Western-style toilets with a special sign on the door (see List of Signs & Inscriptions at the end of the book). If someone knocks at the door, don't panic: it is a way to check whether it's occupied. The right way to respond is to knock back.

The word "bathroom" (*basurūmu*) usually refers to the place where one takes a bath or shower.

A little warning: some facilities do not have toilet paper or towels. Sometimes it is possible to buy them at vending machines at the entrance, but to be on the safe side, it is always better to have your own tissues.

Excuse me, where is the toilet? **Sumimasen, o-tearai-wa doko desu ka?**
toilet **toire** (*generic term*)

Toilets also have a variety of euphemistic names, such as:

**benjo** ("convenience")
**o-tearai** ("hand-washing place")
**semmenjo** ("washroom")
**keshōshitsu** ("powder room")
Japanese style (toilet) **washiki**
Western style (toilet) **yōshiki**
men's room **danshiyō, shinshiyō**
ladies' room **joshiyo, fujin'yō**

building **tatemono, biru**
building number **banchi**
bus stop **basu-no teiryūjo; basutei**
to cross (*a street*) **wataru**
intersection **kōsaten**
map, plan **chizu**
police station **kōban**
square **hiroba**
station (*railway and subway*) **eki**
street **toori**
street corner **kado**
street crossing **ōdan-hodō**
to walk **aruite iku**
underground walkway **chikadō**

straight **massugu**
to the right **migi-e**
to the left **hidari-e**
next to **tonari**
nearby **soba**
behind **ushiro**
in front of **mae**
close (*nearby*) **chikai**
far **tooi**

### In a Building (Biru-no naka-ni)

information desk **annaijo, uketsuke**
entrance **iriguchi**
exit **deguchi**
escalator **esukarētā**
elevator **erebētā**
stairs **kaidan**
to open (*a door*) **hiraku; akeru**
to close (*a door*) **shimeru, tojiru**
open (*stores, restaurants*) **eigyōchū**
closed (*stores, restaurants*) **junjichū, heiten**
out of order (*not working*) **koshō, kyūshi**

## 7. SIGHTSEEING

We'd like to go on a sightseeing tour of the city.
**Watakushitachi-wa shinai-wo kembutsu-
shitai no desu ga.**

Can I see… **…-wo miraremasuka?**

What **museums** (temples, shrines) are there in this
town? **Kono machi-ni-wa donna
*hakubutsukan* (o-tera, jinja)-ga arimasu ka?**

**When** was this building built? **Kono tatemono-
wa *itsu taterareta* no desu ka?**

**What** is in this building? **Kore-wa *dōyū*
tatemono desu ka?**

**Who** is this statue? **Kore-wa *dare-no dōzō* desu ka?**

**What's written** in this inscription? **Kono
hibun(-ni)-wa *nani-ga kakarete* imasu ka?**

We'd like to go to the park to see **cherries** (plums,
peach trees, irises) in blossom. *Sakura* (**ume,
momo, ayame**)-ga saite iru kōen-ni ikitai
no desu.

What's the name of this park? **Kono kōen-wa
nanto iimasu ka?**

When was this **temple** built? **Kono *o-tera* (if
Buddhist; *jinja*, if Shintoist)-wa itsu dekita
no desu ka?**

Is this a **Buddhist temple** or a Shintoist shrine?
**Kore-wa o-tera desu ka? Jinja desu ka?**

To what **sect** of Buddhism does this temple
belong? **Kono o-tera-wa doko-no *shūha*-ni
zokushite iru no desu ka?**

We would like to see the **panoramic view** of the
city. (**Watakushitachi-wa**) *machi-no-zenkei*-
wo mitai no desu ga.

It's so beautiful here! **Koko wa totemo kirei desu ne!**

We **like** your city very much. (**Watakushitachi-wa) kono machi-ga taihen ki-ni** *irimashita/* **daisuki desu.**

## 8. TRAVEL & TRANSPORTATION

### In the City

Public transportation in Tokyo and other big cities includes bus, subway and urban railways. For subway and local trains, tickets are sold by ticket machines, with fare charts nearby. If you cannot read the name of the station you want to go to, buy the cheapest ticket and pay the difference at the fare adjustment machine or window (*seisanjo*) when you exit the station at your destination.

The next station is announced as **Tsugi-wa … de gozaimasu**.

When you need to get off the bus, press the button next to your seat.

How can I get to the Tokyo Tower? **Tokyō tawā-e iku-ni wa /donna norimono-ga arimasu ka/dō ittara ii desu ka?**

**Till** what time is the subway open? **Chikatetsu-wa *nan-ji-made* hashitte imasu ka?**

Can I get there by **subway**? **Soko-e *chikatetsu*-de ikemasu ka?**

**Yes**, it's possible. *Ee*, **ikemasu.**

Where is the (closest) subway **station**? **Chikatetsu-no *eki*-wa doko desu ka?**

Where is the (closest) bus **stop**? **Basu-no *teiryūjo*-wa doko desu ka?**

**Which bus** should I take to get to… **…e iku-ni-wa *dono basu*-de ittara ii deshō ka?**

How long does it take to get there by car? **Soko-e-wa norimono-de dono kurai kakarimasu ka?**

What's the **fare** to Ginza? **Ginza-made ikura desu ka?**

**One** (two) **ticket**(s) to Ginza, please. **Ginza-ichimai (nimai) kudasai.**

Is it **far** to Toranomon station? **Toranomon-eki-made-wa** *tooi* **desu ka?**

Does this train **stop** in Yotsuya? **Kono densha-wa Yotsuya-ni** *tomarimasu* **ka?**

What is the **next** stop? *Tsugi*-**wa doko desu ka?**

Is Shinjuku next? **Tsugi wa Shinjuku desu ka?**

Tell me when we get to the Shibuya station, please. **Shibuya-eki-ni tsuitara oshiete kudasai.**

We are getting off here. **Koko-de orimashō.**

**Taxi (Takushi)**

When you take a taxi, make sure to have the exact address (or better, a map). Don't touch the cab doors: they open and shut automatically. And remember: in Japan tips are not appropriate for either cab drivers or waiters.

Call a cab, please. (*to a hotel or restaurant staff*) **Takushii-wo yonde kudasai.**

To the **railway station**, please. *Eki*-**made onegai shimasu.**

To Narita **Airport**, please. **Narita** *kūkō*-**e itte kudasai.**

Drive me to this **address. Kono** *jūsho* **e o-negai-shimasu.**

Please **stop** over there. **Asoko-de *tomete* kudasai.**

Wait for me here, I'll be right **back. Sugu *modorimasu*-kara, chotto matte kudasai.**

How much do I have to pay? **O-ikura desu ka?**

(*leaving the cab*) **Which way** is Ueno park? **Ueno kōen-wa *docchi* desu ka?**


bus **basu**

bus stop **basu noriba, basu tei(ruijo)**

cab **takushii**

    to call a cab **takushii-wo yobu**

    to take a cab **takushii-wo hirou**

    cab stand **takushii sutando**

direct route **norikae nashi-de, chokutsū**

to get on/to board **noru, jōsha-suru**

to get off **gesha-suru, oriru**

to leave something (in a bus) **(basu-no naka-ni) wasuremono-wo suru**

means of transportation **norimono**

public transportation **kōkyō kōtsu kikan**

rush hour **rasshu awā**

to stop (transitive) **tomeru**; (intransitive) **tomaru**

subway **chikatetsu**

ticket **kippu**

    one (two, three) ticket(s) **kippu ichimai (nimai, sammai)**

train (steam locomotive, long distance) **kisha**; (electric car, commuter) **densha**

train making all stops/local train **hutsū ressha**

tram (street car) **romen densha**

transfer **norikae**

Where does … go? **…doko yuki desu ka?**

## Travel (Ryokō)

Since most travel agents who sell international air-line tickets understand and speak English, information on international air travel is not included in this book. Travelers who wish to take domestic flights, for example from Tokyo to Sapporo or Nagasaki, will easily find English-speaking airline staff.

There are several railway companies in Japan: the biggest is Japanese Railways (commonly known as JR), in addition to Hankyu and other private lines.

## Train (Ressha)

Tickets for out-of-town trains can be bought at ticket windows (*kippu uriba*) at the station. You can buy one-way (*katamichi*) or round-trip (*ōhuku*) tickets. You also have the choice between unreserved (*jiyū sekiken* – "find-yourself-seat") or reserved seat tickets (*shiteisekiken*). The latter is more expensive. First-class tickets (*guriin sha*) are sold at the so-called "Green Windows" (*midori-no madoguchi*).

Excuse me, how do I get to the station?
**Sumimasen ga, eki-e-wa dō ittara ii deshō ka?**
Where is the train schedule? (**Ressha-no**)
*jikokuhyō*-wa doko desu ka?
Where is the ticket office? **Kippu uriba-wa doko desu ka?**

**At the Ticket Window (Kippu uriba)**

**How much** is the one-way fare to Nikko? **Nikko-made katamichi *ikura* desu ka?**

**Two adults'** and one child to Nikko, please. **Nikko-made *otona hutari*, kodomo hitori, kudasai.**

Two **round-trip tickets** to Hiroshima, please. **Hiroshima-made ōhuku *kippu*-wo nimai kudasai.**

How long is this ticket **valid**? **Kono kippu-wa nannichikan *yūkō* desu ka?**

**How long** does the trip to Kyoto take approximately? **Kyōto-made (kisha-de) *nan jikan*-gurai desu ka?**

It takes about **six hours** by express train. **Kyūkō-de iku to *roku jikan*-gurai desu.**

When is the **next train** to Kamakura? **Kamakura-yuki-no *tsugi-no ressha*-wa nan ji desu ka?**

From **what platform** do the trains to Kamakura depart? **Kamakura-yuki-wa *namban hōmu* desu ka?**

**On the Platform (Homu-de)**

From **which side** of the platform does the express train to Osaka leave? **Ōsaka-yuki-no kyūkō-wa /*nambansen*-kara/*dochira gawa*-kara hassha-shimasu ka?**

Is this the express train to Osaka? **Kore-wa Ōsaka-yuki kyūkō desu ka?**

Does this train **stop** in Kamakura? **Kono ressha-wa Kamakura-ni** */teisha-shimasu* **ka** */tomari masu* **ka?**

Does this train **go** to Nagoya? **Kono kisha-wa Nagoya-e** *ikimasu* **ka?**

Yes, it does. **(Hai,) ikimasu.**

You need to make a **transfer**. *Norikae-***nakereba narimasen.**

**On the Train (Shanai-de)**

Is this seat **free** (*not reserved*)? **Kono seki-wa** *aite* **imasu ka?**

No, it's **occupied**. **Iie,** *husagatte* **imasu.**

Excuse me, it's **my seat. Shitsurei desu ga, soko-wa** *watakushi/watashi/-no seki* **desu.**

Do you mind if I **open** (close) a window? **Mado-wo** *aketemo/shimetemo* **iidesu-ka?**

arrival **tōchaku**
air terminal **kūkō tāminaru**
airplane **hikōki**
airport **kūkō**
airport of departure **shuppatsu kūkō**
airport of destination **tōchaku kūkō**
departure **shuppatsu**
passengers' waiting hall **machiaishitsu; robii**

train **kisha, ressha, densha**
limited express train **tokkyū**
express train **kyūkō**
local express train **junkyū**
fast express train **kaisoku**

car (*of a train*) **sharyō**

sleeping car **shindaisha**

conductor **shashō**

first-class car **guriin-sha** ("green car")

Japanese Railway **JR** (reads *jei-āru*)

local train **hutsū ressha**

luggage **nimotsu**

to make a transfer **norikaeru**

platform **hōmu**

porter **akabō**

dining car **shokudōsha**

seat **seki**

seat for elderly and disabled persons **sirubā-siito** ("silver seat")

station/terminal **eki**

station officer **ekiin**

(train, etc.) schedule **jikokuhyō**

ticket **kippu**

　one-way ticket **katamichi kippu**

　round-trip ticket **ōhuku kippu**

　transfer ticket **tōshi kippu**

　to buy a ticket **kippu-wo kau**

　ticket office **kippu uriba**

## 9. COMMUNICATIONS

### Post Office (Yubinkyoku)

Post offices can be identified by a big sign resembling the capital letter T with an additional horizontal stroke above (T̄). Usually they are open Monday–Friday from 9:00 A.M. to 5:00 P.M. and from 9:00 A.M. to 3:00 P.M. on Saturdays. Some bigger offices have a "night window" for special services. Along with standard airmail letters, there are also "aerograms" (*ea retā*) – a kind of folded postcard to send short messages in a more economical way. It is possible (and widely accepted) to send cash in special envelopes that are available at the post office. These are called *genkin kakitome hūtō*.

Where is the nearest post office? **Kono chikaku-no yubinkyoku-wa doko-ni arimasu ka?**

What time does the post office open? **Yūbinkyoku-wa nan ji kara nan ji made desu ka?**

Where can I buy a **letter pad** and envelopes? *Binsen* **to hūtō-wa doko-de kattara ii desho ka/kaemasu ka?**

Give me **stamps** for these letters, please. **Korera-no tegami-ni haru** *kitte*-**wo kudasai.**

Give me ten 80-yen stamps, please. **Hachiju-en kitte-wo jūmai kudasai.**

**Write** this address in Japanese, please. **Kono atena-wo nihongo-de** *kaite* **kudasai.**

I wish to send this by **registered** mail. **Kono tegami-wo** *kakitome*-**ni shite kudasai.**

Send it by express, please. *Sokutatsu*-**de onegai**
   **shimasu.**

I **wish to send** these books as a parcel. **Korera no**
   **hon-wo kozutsumi-*de okutte moraitai* no desu.**

I'd like to send a **parcel**. Where can I do that?
   **Yubin-*kozutsumi*-wa doko-de uketsukete**
   **imasu ka?**

How much is a parcel? **Kozutsumi yubin-wa**
   **ikura desu ka?**

Please help me to **fill in** this money order. **Kawase**
   **yoshi-ni *kinyū-shite* kudasaimasen ka?**

Is there any mail for me (lit: "to my name")?
   **Watakushi ate-no tegami-wa kite imasen**
   **ka/imasuka?**

Please forward all correspondence to this address.
   **Yubinbutsu-wa zenbu kono atena-ni kaisō**
   **shite kudasai.**


address **atena, jūsho**
airmail **kōkūbin**
aerogram **eā retā, kūkan hagaki**
communication **tsūshin, renraku**
envelope **hūtō**
envelope to send cash **genkin kakitome hūtō**
glue (n.) **nori**
letter **tegami**
   registered letter **kakitome**
   certified letter **haitatsu-shōmei yūbin**
   special delivery (express) **sokutatsu**
mail **yūbin**
mailbox (postal) **posuto**
mailbox (individual) **yūbin uke**
main post office **chūō yūbinkyoku**

# COMMUNICATIONS

office window **madoguchi**
letter pad **binsen**
parcel **kozutsumi**
post office **yūbinkyoku**
post office box (P.O.B.) **shishobako**
postal index (zip code) **yūbin bangō**
postcard **hagaki**

**Telephone, Fax (Denwa, Fakkusu)**

Public phones can be operated by 10 or 100-yen coins. In case of an emergency, press the red button at the bottom, and make a toll-free call to the police (110), or the fire department and ambulance (119).

I need to make a phone call. **(Watakushi-wa) denwa-wo kaketai no desu ga.**
**May I use** this phone? **Kono denwa-wo** *tsukatte ii* **deshō ka/mo ii desuka?**
**How** can I use pay phones? **Kōshū denwa-wa** *dōyatte kakeru* **no desu ka?**
How can I make an **overseas** call? *Kokusai* **denwa-wa, dō yatte kakeru no desu ka?**
Hello! **Moshi-moshi.**
This is Clark speaking. **Kochira-wa Kurāku desu.**
Who is calling, please? **Dochira-sama desu ka?**
May I speak to Mr. Suzuki? **Suzuki-san-wo o-negai-shimasu.**
He doesn't answer. **Kotae-ga arimasen.**
He (she) is **not here** now. **Tadaima** *seki-wo hazushite* **imasu/ima imasen.**
Do you want to leave a message? **O-kotozuke-shimashō ka?**

I cannot hear you well. **Yoku kikoemasen.**

The line is busy. **O-hanashichū desu.**

Sorry, wrong number. **Bangō-chigai desu**.

This telephone doesn't work. **Kono denwa-wa koshō desu**.

Would you please speak louder? **Mō sukoshi ōkina koe-de hanashite kudasai/dashite kudasai.**

Hold on please. **Shōshō o-machi kudasai.**

Connect me with an **interpreter**. *Tsūyaku*-wo denwa guchi-ni yobidashite kudasai.

Ask him (her) to call me back. **Watakushi-ni denwa-wo kudasarū yōni o-tsutae-kudasai.**

When (where) can I call you? **Itsu (doko-e) o-denwa-shitara ii desu ka/yoroshii desuka?**

What is your number? **Anata-no denwa-bangō-wa namban desu ka**?

I want to send a fax. **Fakkusu-wo okuritai no desu**.

---

**Young People's Language**

*How are you?* ***Daijōbu?*** *(simple greeting)*

*Are you O.K.?* ***Genki?*** *(expressing some concern)*

*Fine.* ***Genki-dayo*** *(m.)/**-yo** (f.).*

*I want to see you.* ***Anata-ni aitai.***

*I'll miss you.* ***Sabisikunaru yo.***

*I'll call you from New York.* ***Nyū-yōku-kara denwa suru-yo*** *(m.)/**-wa** (f.).*

*I'll be back soon.* ***Sugu kaette-kuru yo*** *(m.)/**wa** (f.).*

---

telephone (abstract term) **denwa**
telephone (machine) **denwaki**

# COMMUNICATIONS

telephone handset **juwaki**

telephone number **denwa bangō**

office number **tsutomesaki-no denwa bangō**

home number **jitaku-no denwa bangō**

public phone **kōshū denwa**

telephone center **denwa kyoku**

telephone directory **denwachō**

to cut the conversation (to hang up) **denwa-wo kiru**

fax **fakkusu**

to send a file (lit.: data) **fairu (dēta) wo okuru**

telegram **dempō**

e-mail **ii-meiru**

## 10. ACCOMMODATION

In most big cities, Japanese hotel staff speaks at least some English. Travelers to the countryside might find the following phrases helpful for communication with innkeepers.

Would you recommend us a budget hotel in **Japanese** (Western) style? **Amari takaku nai** *ryokan* **(hoteru)-wo shōkai-shite kudasai.**

In which hotel shall we stay? **(Watakushitachi-wa) dono hoteru-ni tomaru no deshō ka/tomarimashō ka?**

We would like to stay in the **center** of the city. **(Watakushitachi-wa) machi-no** *chūshin*-**ni tomaritai no desu ga.**

Give me the **address** of that hotel, please. **Hoteru-no** *jūsho*-**wo kudasai.**

Could you write the address, please. **Jūsho-wo kaite kudasai.**

Excuse me, what's the way to the **Imperial** Hotel? **Sumimasen ga,** *Teikoku*-**hoteru-wa doko desho ka?**

Do you have vacancies? **Aita heya-ga arimasu ka?**

Is there a telephone (air-conditioning)? **Heya-ni denwa (eakon)-wa arimasu ka?**

How much is this room for one night? **Kono heya-wa hitoban ikura desu ka?**

We booked a room through a **travel agency**. *Ryokōsha*-**wo tsujite heya-wo yoyaku-shita no desu ga.**

I'll take this room. **Kono heya-de kekko desu.**

May I have the key? **Kagi-wo kudasai.**

Should we take off our shoes? **Koko-wa kutsu-wo nuganakereba ikemasen ka.**

Take my **hand luggage** to the room, please. *Tenimotsu*-wo (watakushi-no) heya-ni motte-kite kudasai.

Send this underwear to the **laundry** (dry cleaning), please. **Kono shitagi-wo** *sentaku* (kuriiningu)-ni dashite kudasai.

When can I have it back? **Itsu dekimasu ka?**

I need it sooner. *Motto hayaku* o-negai shimasu.

It's urgent. **Isogimasu/Isogidesu.**

I'd like to have breakfast (supper) in my room. **(Watakushi-wa) chōshoku (yūshoku)-wo heya-de tabetai no desu ga.**

What is Yanagi's room number? **Yanagi-san-wa** *nangōshitsu* **deshō ka?**

The TV set doesn't work. **Terebi-ga koshō-shite imasu.**

The bill, please. **Kanjōgaki-wo kudasai.**

Call a cab, please. **Kuruma-wo/Takushii-wo yonde kudasai.**


hotel (Western-style) **hoteru**

hotel (Japanese-style) **ryokan**

room **heya**

single room **hitoribeya**

double room **hutaribeya**

to book a room **heya-wo yoyaku-suru**

key **kagi**

travel agency **ryokōsha**

room service **rūmu-sābisu**

maid **mēdo-san**

receptionist (front desk) **furonto**

bill **kanjō gaki**

## 11. FOOD & DRINK

In many restaurants, plastic samples of dishes are displayed in the window. Sometimes the menu has color photos of dishes. In these cases, the easiest way to order is to point to the dish and say **Kore-wo kudasai**. Sushi parlors (*shushiya*) have either plastic samples or photos. At a **kaiten-zushi** ("belt sushi shop"), tiny plates are moving on a conveyer belt and you simply take what you would like to eat.

Places to have a drink are bars (*bā*), pubs (*pabu*) or *izakaya*, usually relatively cheap and unpretentious drinking parlors.

I'm hungry. **(Watakushi-wa) o-naka-ga sukimashita.**

Have you had your **lunch** already? *Hirugokan*-**wa o-sumi-ni narimashita ka**/*Chūshoku* **wa mō sumimashita ka?**

Not yet. **Iie, mada desu.**

Let's have **breakfast** (dinner, supper) somewhere. *Dokokade asa-gohan* (**hiru-gohan, ban-gohan**)-**wo tabemashō.**

Do they have **European** (Japanese) **cuisine** here? **Kochira-wa** *seiyō ryōri* (**nihon ryōri**) **desu ka?**

Are you **alone**? (meaning: "A table for two?") (*waiter's question at the entrance*) **O-hitori desu ka?**/*O-hutari* **desu ka?**

Bring me the menu, please. **Menyū-wo kudasai.**

What do you like to eat? **Nani-wo meshiagari masu ka?**

Choose for us, please. **Kawarini erande kudasai.**

Bring us a dinner of **Japanese dishes**. **Ban-gohan-wa** *nihon ryōri*-**ni shite kudasai.**

I am a vegetarian. **Watakushi-wa saishokushugi desu.**

For religious reasons, I am a vegetarian. And I cannot eat food which contains certain ingredients or is prepared with these ingredients. **Shūkyōjō-no riyū de, saishokushugi desu. Tokutei-no himmoku-wo hukunda mono ya, sore-wo tsukatte chōri-sareta mono-wa, taberaremasen.**

None of the food can contain any meat or meat products. **Niku (ryōri) to niku seihin-wa taberaremasen.**

None of the food should contain any fish or seafood. **Gyokairui-wa taberaremasen.**

All fish or seafood must be scaly fish (lit.: "must have had scales when alive"). **Gyokairui-wa uroko-ga aru mono shika taberaremasen.**

I'd like to take this. **Kore-wo kudasai.**

I'd like to try **this dish. (Watakushi-wa)** *kono ryōri*-wo tabete mitai no desu.

I'd like my steak **well-done**, please. **Suteiki-wa** *ueru-dan*-wo/*yoku yaite* **kudasai.**

Shall we **drink** something? **Nani-ka** *nomimashō* **ka?**

Do you want a glass of **red** (white) **wine?** *Aka budōshu/shiro budōshu* **ippai ikaga desu ka?**

May I fill your glass? **O-tsugi-shimashō.**

**No, thanks**, I had enough. *Iie, kekkō* **desu. Mō jūbun desu.**

I would like to have a **beer.** *Biiru*-wo itadakimashō.

Give me a **fork**, please. *Fōku*-wo kudasai.

I cannot eat with **chopsticks. (Watakushi-wa)** *o-hashi*-ga tsukaemasen.

Show me **how** to hold chopsticks, please.

    **O-hashi-wa** *dōyūfu-ni* **tsukaimasu ka?**

Waiter! (lit.: excuse me!) **Sumimasen!**

Bring me … **…-wo motte-kite kudasai.**

| | |
|---|---|
| …some fruits. | **Kudamono…** |
| …ice cream. | **Aisu-kuriimu…** |
| …mineral water. | **Mineraru wōtā…** |
| …sake. | **Sake…** |
| …coffee. | **Kōhii…** |
| …cigarettes. | **Tabako…** |

Will you pass me the **salt**? **(Dozo)** *shio*-**wo**

    *totte/mawashite* **kudasaimasen ka?**

The bill, please.(Lit.: How much is it?) **O-ikura**

    **desu ka?**

---

**Young People's Language**

*I'm hungry.* **Onaka-ga suita.**

*I'm thirsty.* **Nodo-ga kawaita.**

*Do you want to eat?* **Tabetai/Taberu?**

*I want to grab something.* **Nanka tabetai.**

*I don't want to eat.* **Tabetakunai.**

*Did you have your lunch?* **Ohiru tabeta?**

*How about some dinner?* **Shokuji shinai?**

*What would you like?* **Nani-ga hoshii?**

*I'd like some beer.* **Biiru-ga nomitai.**

*Do you want to drink something?* **Nanka nomu?**

*I won't drink.* **Nomanai.**

*Will you try this?* **Kore tabete miru?**

*What's that?* **Nani sore?**

*What's it called?* **Nante iu-no?**

*Smells good.* **Ii nioi.**

*Looks delicious.* **Oishisō.**

**Young People's Language** (*continued*)
*Enough?* **Tarita?**
*Enough!* **Ippai!**
*Is this tasty?* **Kore oishii?**
*I can't eat this.* **Sore taberarenai.**
*Not good.* **Oishikunai.**
*It's awful.* **Mazui.**
*I like it.* **Suki.**
*I hate it.* **Dai kirai.**

ashtray **haizara**
bill **o-kanjō**
cashier **rejii**
chopsticks **hashi**
fork **fōku**
glass **koppu, gurasu**
knife **naifu**
napkin **napukin**
plate **sara**
spoon **supūn**
wet towel **o-shibori**

strong **koi; tsuyoi** (alcohol)
weak **usui; yowai** (alcohol)
sweet **amai**
sour **suppai**
bitter **nigai**
spicy, hot **karai**
hot **atsui**
cold **tsumetai**
delicious **oishii, umai** (*men*)

to be thirsty **nodo-ga kawaku**
to be hungry **o-naka-ga suku**
to be full **ippai**

steak **sutēki**
hamburger **hāmbāgu**
consommé **konsome**
sandwich **sandoitchi**
cheese sandwich **chiizu-sandoitchi**
ham sandwich **hamu-sandoitchi**
meat prepared at the table **sukiyaki**
slices of beef dipped in boiling water **shabu-shabu**
ginger **shōga**
potato **poteto, jagaimo**
rice with curry **karē-raisu**

fish **sakana**
raw fish **sashimi**
horseradish **wasabi**
egg **tamago**

juice **jūsu**
water **mizu**
coca cola **koka-kōra**
tea **o-cha (cha)**
    green tea **ryoku cha**
    black tea **kōcha**
    tea with lemon **remon tii**
    tea with milk **miruku tii**
    iced tea **aisu tii**
coffee **kōhii**
sake **sake**
beer **biiru**

vodka **uokka**

wine **wain, budō-shu**

    white wine **shiro budōshu**

    red wine **aka budōshu**

cognac **kon'yak**

champagne **shampan**

## 12. SHOPPING

Most department stores (***depato***) are open from 10:00 A.M. to 6:00 P.M., six days a week, including Sunday. The day off can be Monday or another day (different for each store). There are directories (sometimes bilingual) in many big stores and supermarkets (***sūpā***). In most stores floor plans in English are available at the information counter (***annai***). Usually, the food section is in the basement; accessories and various small items are on the first floor, and children's, women's, and men's clothing, as well as household goods and furniture can be found on the upper floors. On the last floor there are usually restaurants and cafes (this floor is open until late). Big department stores often have their own art gallery, with exhibitions from the best museums in Europe and North America. On the roof there might be children's playgrounds and places to sit down and relax.

Sales assistants in department stores usually know some English. In other cases the easiest way to communicate is to point to the item you want and say:

Show me this, please. **Kore-wo misete kudasai.**
I'll take this. **Kore-wo kaitai no desu ga.**

I'm just looking. **Chotto miru dake.**
**How much** is this? **Kore-wa *ikura* desu ka?**
I need something **cheaper** (more expensive).
    **(Watakushi-wa) motto *yasui* (takai) no ga
    hoshii no desu.**

How much do I have to pay **in total**? *Zembu-de* **ikura-ni naru n desu ka/narimasu ka?**

Could you please write down the **price**? *Nedan*-wo **kaite kudasai.**

I'd like to think about it a little more (*polite refusal*). **Mō sukoshi kangaete mimasu.**

### Department Store (Depāto)

I need to buy something. **(Watakushi-wa) kaimono-wo shinakereba narimasen.**

I'd like to go to a **department store. (Watakushi-wa)** *depāto*-e ikitai (no) desu (ga).

Where is the nearest department store? **Kono chikaku-no depāto-wa doko desu ka?**

### In a Store

Excuse me. Where are the… **Sumimasen. …-wa doko desu ka?**

May I see this? **Sore-wo misete kudasai.**

**How much** is this? **Kore-wa** *ikura* **desu ka?**

It's **expensive.** *Takai* **desu ne.**

Show me **100% silk**, please. *Honken*-wo **misete kudasai.**

Is there any other **design**? **Betsuno** *gara*-wa **arimasen ka?**

Are there other **colors** (styles)? **Betsuno** *iro* **(stairu)-wa arimasen ka?**

Show me **suits** (dresses, pants, skirt) that would fit me, please. **Watakushi-no au yona** *yōhuku* **(doresu, zubon, sukāto)-wo misete kudasai.**

May I try it on? **Kite mite mo ii desu ka?**

Where is the **dressing room**? *Shichakushitsu*-wa
doko desu ka?

I need one size **bigger** (smaller). **(Watakushi –wa)**
*hito mamari ōkii* (chiisai) no-ga hoshii no desu.

It's **fitting well.** Kore-wa *pittari* desu.

It doesn't suit me. **Kore-wa aimasen.**

I need men's (ladies', children's) **underwear.**
**Danshiyō (hujin'yō, kodomoyō)-no** *shitagi*-ga
hoshii no desu-ga.

What **size** is this? **Nan** *saizu* desu ka?

Show me men's (ladies', children's) **shoes,** please.
**Danshiyō (hujin'yō, kodomoyō)-no** *kutsu*-wo
misete kudasai.

I need **size…** (Watakushi-wa)… *saizu*-ga hoshii
no desu.

May I try this on? (*about footwear*)  **Chotto haite
mitemo ii desu ka?**

Show me **summer** (winter) shoes. *Natsu*
(huyu)-no kutsu-wo misete kudasai.

May I try this hat on? **Kabutte mite mo ii desu ka?**


**Camera Shop (Kameraya)**


I'd like to buy a camera (camcorder).
**(Watakushi-wa) kamera (kamucōdā)-wo
kaitai no desu ga.**

Is this camera made in **Japan**? **Kono kamera-wa**
*nihonsei* desu ka?

Who is the **manufacturer** of this camera? **Kono
kamera no** *mēka* wa?

Is there an **English manual**? *Eibun-no
setsumeisho*-wa arimasu ka?

**How much** is this camera? **Kono kamera-wa**
*ikura* desu ka?

I'd like to have this film **developed**. (**Watakushi-wa**) **firumo-no** *genzō*-wo **shite moraitai no desu ga.**

When it is ready? **Itsu dekimasu ka?**

**Buying Souvenirs (O-miyage wo kau)**

I'd like to buy some **souvenirs.** *O-miyage*-wo **kaitai no desu ga.**

Show me traditional Japanese **toys** (dolls), please. **Nihon no mingei** *omocha* (**ningyō**)-wo **misete kudasai.**

Who is the **manufacturer** of this watch? **Kono tokei-no mēkā wa doko desu ka?**

I'd like to buy Japanese **lacquerware.** (**Watakushi-wa**) *urushi*-nuri no **mingeihin-wo kaitai no desu ga.**

   … ivory.      **…zōge…**

   … silver.     **…gin…**

   … rice straw.  **…wara…**

What **material** is this? **Kore-wa** *nan-de tsukutta mono* **desu ka?**

I'd like to buy a Japanese **tea set.** (**Watakushi-wa**) *chaki setto*-wo **kaitai no desu ga.**

Show me **teacups** with traditional designs, please. **Dentōteki-na moyō-no tsuita** *chawan*-wo **misete kudasai.**

How much is this **cup**? **Kono** *chawan*-wa **ikura desu ka?**

Isn't it a little **expensive**? **Sukoshi** *nedan-ga harimasu* **ne?**

Do you have **cheaper** items? *Motto yasui* **no-wa arimasen ka?**

Would you please **wrap** it up? *Zembu issho-ni tsutsunde* **kudasai.**

# SHOPPING

## In a Bookstore (Hon'ya de)

I'd like to visit a second-hand **bookstore.**
(**Watakushi-wa**) *huruhon'ya*-**ni ikitai no
desu.**

Where are there second-hand bookstores?
**Huruhon'ya-wa doko desu ka?**

I'm interested in books in **English** (Japanese, Chinese). (**Watakushi-wa**) *eigo*-**no (nihongo-no,
chugokugo-no) hon-ga hoshii no desu.**

Where can I buy books about **art history**
(sports, languages)? *Bijutsu-shi* (**supōtsu,
gengogaku**)-**ni kansuru hon-wa doko-de utte
imasu ka?**

Show me **children's** books, please. *Kodomo-no*
**tame-no hon-wo misete kudasai.**

How much is this book? **Kono hon-wa ikura
desu ka?**

Where is a **newsstand**? *Shimbun-uriba*-**wa doko
deshō ka?**

Give me *The Japan Times* of today, please. **Kyō-no
Japan taimusu-wo kudasai.**

## At the Optician (Meganeya de)

Where can I order **glasses**? *Megane*-**wa doko-de
atsuraerare masu ka?**

My glasses **need repair**. (**Watakushi-wa**)
**megane-wo** *naoshite moraitai* **no desu.**

Choose a pair of glasses for me, please.
(**Watakushi-ni**) **au megane-wo erande
kudasai.**

I'm **nearsighted** (farsighted). **Watakushi-wa**
*kinshi* (**enshi**) **desu.**

I need **sunglasses**. **Watakushi-wa** *san gurasu ga* **hoshii no desu.**

May I see **that one**, please? **Are wo misete kudasai.**

**Grocery (Shokuryō hinten)**

Where is the nearest **grocery**? **Kono chikaku-no** *shokuryo hinten*-**wa doko desu ka?**

Where can I buy **fruits**? *Kudamono*-**wa doko de kaemasu ka?**

...vegetables? **Yasai...**

...meat? **Niku...**

...fish? **Sakana...**

Is this **fish** (meat) fresh? **Kono sakana (niku)-wa** *shinsen* **desu ka?**

Show me this, please. **Kore-wo misete kudasai.**

Is there a **candy store** nearby? **Kono chikaku ni** *kashiya*-**wa arimasu ka?**

I'd like to buy Japanese **candies** and **pastries**. **(Watakushi-wa)** *o-kashi*-**wo kaitai no desu ga.**

I want to buy a **bottle of sake**. **(Watakushi-wa)** *sake*-**wo ippon kaitai no desu ga.**

Which brand of sake is the **best**? **Dore ga** *ichiban* **iidesu ka?**

Give me a bottle of beer (juice). **Biiru (jūsu)-wo ippon kudasai.**

What's the total? **Zembu-de ikura desu ka?**

**Shops (Ya, Ten)**

bakery **pan'ya**
barber **tokoya**

beauty parlor **biyōin**

bookstore **hon'ya**

clothing store **yōhukuya, yō hinten**

department store **depāto**

drugstore/pharmacy **kusuriya**

electric appliance store **denkiya**

furniture store **kaguya**

fruit store **kudamonoya**

greengrocer **yaoya**

grocery **sūpā (māketto), shokuryohin'ya**

liquor store **sakaya**

photo shop **kamera'ya**

second-hand store **risaikuru shoppu**

shoe store **kutsuya**

shopping mall **shoppingu sentā**

underground shopping area **chikagai**

bargain **bāgen**

change **otsuri**

counter **uriba**

to exchange **torikaeru**

on sale **sēru, bāgen**

receipt **ryōshūsho**

sample **mihon**

special price **tokka**

to wrap up **tsutsumu**

book **hon**

journal/magazine **zasshi**

newspaper **shimbun**

pencil **empitsu**

### Clothes (Irui)

Japanese clothing **wahuku**
Western clothing **yōhuku**
children's apparel **kodomohuku**
ladies' apparel **hujinhuku**
men's apparel **shinshihuku**
dress **doresu**
pants **zubon**
jeans **jiinzu**
jacket **uwagi; sebiro**
men's suit **shinshiyō-sutsu**
women's suit **tsūpiisu** ("two piece"), **sūtsu**
overcoat **obā (koto)**
raincoat **renkōto**
skirt **sukāto**
sweater **sētā**
underwear **shitagi**

### Shoes (Kutsu)

men's shoes **shinshiyō-no kutsu**
women's shoes **hujin'yō-no kutsu**
sandals **sandaru**
slippers **surippa**
traditional Japanese wooden sandals **geta**
socks **sokkusu**
Japanese socks **tabi**

### Food (Tabemono)

bread **pan**
butter **batā**

canned food **kanzume**
caviar **kyabia**
cheese **chiizu**
crab **kani**
egg **tamago**
fish **sakana**
    cuttlefish **ika**
    eel **unagi**
    flounder **hirame**
    gizzard shad **kohada**
    herring **nishin**
    mackerel **saba**
    octopus **tako**
    prawn **taishō ebi**
    red (salmon) roe **ikura**
    roe **harago**
    sardine **iwashi**
    scallop **hotategai**
    shrimp **ko ebi**
    tuna **maguro**
meat **niku**
    beef **gyūniku**
    lamb **hitsuji**
    pork **butaniku**
    ham **hamu**
    sausage **sōsēji**
milk **gyūnyū, miruku**
noodles  (flour) **udon**; (buckwheat) **soba**
olive oil **oriibu oiru**
rice (cooked) **raisu, gohan;** (white uncooked)
    **hakumai**
salt **shio, shyokuen**
sugar **satō**

**Fruits and Vegetables (Kudamono to Yasai)**

apple **ringo**
apricot **anzu**
banana **banana**
cabbage **kyabetsu**
carrot **ninjin**
cherry **sakurambo**
cauliflower **karifurawā**
cucumber **kyūri**
garlic **ninniku**
grapes **budō**
lemon **remon**
tangerine **mikan**
melon **meron**
mushrooms **kinoko**
onion **tamanegi**
orange **orenji**
peach **momo**
pear **nashi**
persimmon **kaki**
pineapple **painappuru**
plum **sumomo**
potato **potato, jagaimo**
radish **akakabu**
tomato **tomato**
turnip **kabu**
scallion **naganegi**
watermelon **suika**
white radish **daikon**

## 13. HEALTHCARE

In Tokyo there are a number of clinics run by foreigners and expatriate private practitioners. Listings might be found through the hotel staff or in English-language telephone directories. People who know little Japanese might prefer to deal with Japanese doctors who understand some English or German, even if they are not so proficient. The proper form of addressing a doctor is *sensei*.

I do not feel **good. (Watakushi-wa)** *kibun-ga warui* **no desu.**

I am **sick. Watakushi-wa** *byoki* **desu.**

Call a **doctor**, please. **O-*isha*-san-wo yonde kudasai.**

Call an **ambulance** immediately. **Shikyū/sugu,** *kyūkyūsha*-**wo yonde kudasai.**

I need to see a **doctor for internal medicine. Watakushi-wa** *naika*-**i-ni mite moraitai no desu.**

　surgeon **geka-i**

　dentist **haisha**

　gynecologist **fujinka-i**

When are the doctor's hours? **O-isha-san-no shinryō jikan-wa itsu desu ka?**

　ambulance **kyūkyūsha**

　examination **shinsatsu**

　hospital **byōin**

　injection **chūsha**

　operation **shujutsu**

　test **kensa**

　symptoms **shōjō**

　X-ray **rentogen**

**At the Doctor's (Shinsatsu)**

(*Doctor*) What's wrong? (Lit.: "Where is a **bad**"?)
**Doko-ga o-*warui* no desu ka?**

(*Doctor*) Where does it **hurt**? **Doko-ga *itai* no
desu ka?**

It **hurts** here. **Koko-ga *itai* desu.**

I have a **fever**. **Watakushi-wa *netsu*-ga arimasu.**
…heart condition. …**dōki.**

I have a **headache. Watakushi-wa *atama-ga itai*
desu.**

| | |
|---|---|
| …I have a stomachache. | …**onaka-ga itai…** |
| …I have a sore throat. | …**nodo-ga itai…** |
| …I have heart pain. | …**shinzō-ga itai…** |

I have **diarrhea. Watakushi-wa *geri wo shite
imasu.***

(*Doctor*) What kind of **pain** is it? **Donna *itami*
desu ka?**

I feel **acute** pain. *Hageshii* **itami desu.**
…dull… **Nibui…**

I have a **cough. Watakushi-wa *seki*-ga demasu.**
…cold. …**kaze…**

I feel like **vomiting** /I am **nauseous. Watakushi-wa
*hakike*-ga shimasu.**

I feel that I have a **fever.** *Netsuppoi* **desu.**

I am suffering from **insomnia.** *Huminshō*-**ni
kakatte imasu.**

I have **a ringing in my ears.** *Miminari*-**ga shimasu.**

I have no appetite. **Shokuyoku-ga arimasen.**

Measure my **blood pressure**, please. *Ketsuatsu*-**wo
hakatte kudasai.**

(*Doctor*) You need to have a **blood test. Anata-wa
ketsueki-kensa-wo /shinakereba narumasen/
suru hitsuyō ga arimasu.**

urine test **nyō kensa**

feces test **ieki-kensa**

blood transfusion **yuketsu**

**How long** will the treatment take? **Chiryo-wa** *nan-nichi* **kakarimasu ka?**

What kind of **medication** should I take? **Donna** *kusuri*-wo **nomeba ii deshō ka?**

**How much** do I have to pay for a visit? **Shinsatsuryō-wa o-***ikura* **desu ka?**


## At the Dentist's (Shika-i)

I have a **toothache.** **(Watakushi-wa)** *ha*-ga itai no desu.

It seems I have a **cavity.** **Mushiha ga asurashii desu.**

(*Dentist*) Your tooth needs a **filling.** *Tsumemon*-wo **suru hitsuyō ga arimasu.**

(*Dentist*) Your tooth needs to be **extracted. Ha-wo** *nuka*nakereba narimasen yo.


## At the Pharmacy (Kusuriya-de)

Excuse me, is there a pharmacy nearby? **Sumimasen, kono chikaku-ni kusuriya-wa arimasen ka?**

Could you please give me a medication for this prescription? **Kono shohōsen-no kusuri-wo chōgō kudasai.**

**When** is the medication ready? **Kusuri-wa** *itsu* **dekimasu ka?**

(*Answer*) Right now. **Sugu dekimasu.**

Give me **a cold medication,** please. *Kaze-gusuri*-wo kudasai.

| | |
|---|---|
| ...cough medicine. | **Seki-dome...** |
| ...painkiller. | **Chintsū-zai...** |
| ...headache medicine. | **Zutsu-no kusuri...** |
| ...stomachache medicine. | **I-no kusuri/ ichō-yaku...** |
| ...laxative. | **Gezai...** |
| ...medicine against diarrhea. | **Geridome...** |

**How** should I **take** this medication? **Kono kusuri-wa** *itsu nomu* **no desu ka?**

**Write** down the instructions, please. **Setsumei-wo** *kaite* **kudasai.**

physician, doctor **isha, ishi, o-isha san**
   dentist **shika, haisha**
   dermatologist **hihuka-no sensei**
   gynecologist **hujinka-i**
   oculist **ganka-i**
   oncologist **shuyōka-i**
   orthopedist **seikeigeka-i**
   pediatrician **shōnika-i**
   surgeon **geka-i**
   therapist **serapisto**
   internist **naika-i**
   urologist **hinyōkika-i**
   nurse **kangohu**
illness **byōki**
   appendicitis **mōchōen; chūsuien**
   blow **dabokushō**
   cerebral hemorrhage **nōikketsu**
   diabetes **tōnyōbyō**
   dysentery **sekiri**
   fever **netsu**

gastritis **i-kataru**

heart failure **shinzōmahi**

influenza **ryūkan**

infectious disease **densenbyō**

be injured **kega-wo surū**

be itchy **kayui**

neuralgia **shinkeitsu**

poisoning **chūdoku**

pleurisy **rokumakuen**

pneumonia **haien**

sclerosis **dōmyaku-kōka**

stomachache **itsū**

normal (temperature) **heinetsu**

wound **husho, kizu**

body **jintai, karada**

side **wakihara**

back **senaka**

arm **ude**

belly/abdomen **hara; onaka**

blood **chi, ketsueki**

bladder **bōkō**

bone **hone**

breast **mune**

buttocks **shiri**

elbow **hiji**

eye **me**

face **kao**

finger **yubi**

forehead **hitai**

genitals **seishokuki**

gum **haguki**

hair **kami**

hand **te**

head **atama**
heart **shinzo**
kidney **jinzō**
knee **hiza**
leg/foot **ashi**
lip **kuchibiru**
liver **kanzō**
lung **hai**
mouth **kuchi**
muscle **kinniku**
nerve **shinkei**
nose **hana**
organism **yūkibutsu**
shoulder **kata**
skin **hihu**
stomach **i**
tongue **shita**
tooth **ha**
waist **koshi**
medicine **kusuri**
medication **tōyaku**
alcohol **arukōru**
ampoule **ampuru**
antibiotics **kōsei-busshitsu**
aspirin **asupirin**
band-aid **bando-eido**
bandage **hōtai**
contraceptive pills **piru, hininyaku**
needle **hari**
pills **jōzai**
prescription **shohōsen**
syringe **chūsyaki**
tampon **tampakkusu**

tranquilizer **chinseizai**
before a meal **shokuzen-ni**
after a meal **shokugo-ni**
at bedtime **neru mae-ni**

## 14. MONEY

Money exchanges can be found in airports and hotels.
Most banks also provide an exchange office on their
second floor. Perhaps the most convenient for foreigners is Citibank, because it is relatively easy to
open an account there and to use its bilingual ATM.

Where is the nearest **bank**? *Ginkō*-wa doko desu ka?
I need to **exchange** dollars for yen. **(Watakushi-wa)**
    **doru-wo en-ni** *kae*neba narimasen/*kae*tai
    nodesuga.
Would you please give me **change** for this?
    *Komakaku*-shite kudasai.
I need smaller bills. **Komakaku-shite kudasai/**
    **Kozeni ga irimasu.**
I'd like to open an account. **Kōza-wo hirakitai no**
    **desu ga.**
I would like to cash this traveler's check.
    **Toraberāzu chiekku wo genkin ni kaetai no**
    **desu ga.**
Show me how to use the cash machine, please.
    **Kyasshu mashin-no tsukaikata-wo oshiete**
    **kudasai.**

bank **ginkō**
bank branch **(ginkō) shiten**
savings account **hutsū yokin**
ATM **kyasshu kōnā** ("cash corner")
money **o-kane, kahei**
cash **genkin**
bills **shihei**
coins **kōka**

change (n.) **o-tsuri**

foreign exchange **gaikoku kawase**

large bills **ookina o-kane**

small bills/coins **chiisana o-kane**

traveler's check **toraberāzu chekku**

credit card **kurejitto kādo**

one yen **ichi en**

ten yen **jū en**

hundred yen **hyaku en**

five hundred yen **gohyaku en**

thousand yen **sen en**

ten thousand yen **ichiman en**

## 15. TALKING ABOUT YOURSELF

**Home (Sumai)**

Where do you live? **Dochira-ni o-sumai desu ka?**

I live in New York (Tokyo). **Nyū-yōku (Tokyō)-ni sunde imasu.**

I live in (the) …district on … street. **…ku …machi-ni sunde imasu.**

Tell me your **address**, please. **Anata-no *jūsho*-wo oshiete kudasai.**

Is your neighborhood quiet? **O-taku-no kinjo-wa kansei/shizuka desu ka?**

No, pretty noisy. **Iie, sōzōshii/urusai desu.**

Yes, very quiet. **Hai, totemo shizuka desu.**

address **atesaki, jūsho**
street **toori**
block **machi**
house number **banchi**
apartment **apāto, jūtaku**
rent **yachin**
room **heya**
bedroom **shinshitsu**
study **shosai**
children's room **kodomobeya**
living room **ribingu rūmu**
guest room **kyakuma**
dining room **shokudo**
kitchen **daidokoro, kitchin**
bathroom **basu-rūmu, o-huro, yokushitsu**
toilet **toire, senmenjo, o-tearai**

# TALKING ABOUT YOURSELF

### Family (Kazoku)

What's your name? **O-namae wa?**

How **big** is your family? **Go-kazoku-wa** *nannin* **desu ka?**

Do you have children? **(Anata-ni-wa) o-ko-san-wa imasu ka?**

How many children do you have? **O-ko-san-wa nannin desu ka?**

How old are your children? **Kodomo-san-wa/ O-ko-san-wa o-ikutsu desu ka?**

Where do your children study? **Kodomo-san-no gakko-wa dochira desu ka?**

My children are already **grown-up**. **Watakushi-no kodomo-wa mō** *otona* **desu.**

I don't have a family. **Watakushi-ni-wa kazoku-ga arimasen.**

I have a big family. **Uchi-wa daikazoku desu.**

I have **two children**: a son and a daughter. **Watakushi-no** *kodomo-wa* **hutari-de musuko to musume desu.**

Are you married? **Anata-wa kekkon-shite irasshaimasu ka?**

Yes, I'm married. **Ee, (watakushi-wa) kekkon-shite imasu.**

I'm single. **Watakushi-wa dokushin desu/ Watakushi-wa mikon desu.**

I'm divorced. **Watakushi-wa rikon shimashita.**

I'm a widower. **Watakushi-wa tsuma-wo ushinaimashita (or nakushimashita.)**

I live with my **parents**. **Watakushi-wa** *ryōshin*-**to isshoni sunde imasu.**

This is my wife (husband). **Watakushi-no tsuma (otto) desu.**

# TALKING ABOUT YOURSELF

**Age (Nenrei)**

How old are you? **Anata-wa o-ikutsu desu ka?**

I'm twenty (thirty, forty). **Watakushi-wa nijū (sanjū, yonjū) ssai desu.**

We are of the same age. **Watakushitachi-wa onaji toshi desu.**

You look younger than your age. **Anata-wa toshiyori wakaku miemasu ne.**

When is your birthday? **Anata-no tanjōbi-wa itsu desu ka?**

How old is your child? **Kodomo-san-wa o-ikutsu desu ka?**

He is an elderly person. **Kare-wa mō toshi desu.**


name **o-namae**

surname and given name **seimei**

maiden name **kekkonmae-no namae**

married name **kekkongo-no namae**

family **kazoku**

big family **daikazoku**

small family **shōkazoku**

single **dokushin**

orphan **minashigo; koji**

husband (*general term*) **otto**

husband (*of the 2nd and 3rd person*) **go-shujin**

husband (*of the 1st person*) **shujin, uchinohito**

wife (*general term*) **tsuma**

wife (*of the 2nd and 3rd person*) **okusan**

wife (*of the 1st person*) **kanai, nyōbō**

child/children **kodomo, o-ko-san**

baby **aka-chan**

son **musuko**

oldest son **chōnan**
second son **jinan**
daughter **musume**
oldest daughter **chōjo**
second daughter **jijo**
adopted child *(m.)* **yōshi**; *(f.)* **yōjo**
stepchild **mamako**
grandchild **mago**
granddaughter **magomusume**
birthday **tanjōbi**
relative **shinseki**
parents **ryōshin**
    father **chichioya, otōsan, chichi**
    mother **hahaoy, okāsan, haha**
    grandpa **o-jiisan, sofu**
    grandma **o-bāsan, sobo**
stepfather **mamachichi**
stepmother **mamahaha**
brother(s) **kyōdai**
    older brother **ani, oniisan**
    younger brother **otōto**
sister(s) **shimai**
    older sister **ane, onēsan**
    younger sister **imōto**
uncle **oji**
aunt **oba**
to marry **kekkon-suru**
wedding **kekkon-shiki**
honeymoon **hanemūn, shinkon**
divorce **rikon**
to divorce **rikon-suru**

# TALKING ABOUT YOURSELF

**Nationality (Kokuseki)**

I'm … **Watakushi-wa…**

…American. **…amerika-jin desu.**

…Australian. **…ōsutoraria-jin desu.**

…British. **…eikokujin desu.**

…Canadian. **…kanada-jin desu.**

…Chinese. **…chūgoku-jin desu.**

…Dutch. **…oranda-jin desu.**

…English. **…igirisu-jin desu.**

…French. **…furansu-jin desu.**

…German. **…doitsu-jin desu.**

…Hispanic. **…raten-kei desu.**

…Indian. **…indo-jin desu.**

…Iranian. **…iran-jin desu.**

…Israeli. **…isuraeru-jin desu.**

…Italian. **…itaria-jin desu.**

…Russian. **…rosia-jin desu**.

…Scottish. **…sukottorando-jin desu.**

I'm an American citizen. **Watakushi-wa Amerika-no shimin/kokumin desu.**

My home country is… **Watakushi-no kokyō-wa…**

…America. **…Amerika desu.**

…Russia. **…Rosia desu.**

…Great Britain. **…Eikoku desu.**

…Germany. **…Doitsu desu.**

…Israel. **…Isuraeru desu.**

Are you Japanese? **Anata-wa Nihonjin desu ka?**

What (where) is your country of birth? **Do no kumi de umaremashita ka?**

What is your home country? **Anata-no kokyō-wa doko desu ka?**

Where do you live? **Anata-wa doko-ni sunde imasu ka?**

I live in New York. **Watakushi-wa Nyū-yōku-ni sunde imasu.**

### Religion (Shūkyō)

I'm Christian. **Watakushi-wa kirisuto-kyōto desu.**

I'm Catholic. **Watakushi-wa katorikku-kyōto desu.**

I'm Protestant. **Watakushi-wa purotestanto(-kyōto) desu.**

I'm Russian (Greek) Orthodox. **Watakushi-wa roshia (girisha) sei-kyōto desu.**

I'm Jewish. **Watakushi-wa yudaya-kyōto desu.**

I'm Muslim. **Watakushi-wa isuramu-kyōto desu.**

Is there a church nearby? **Kono chikaku-ni kyōkaī-wa arimasen ka?**

I have a great interest in **Buddhism** (Shintoism). **Watakushi-wa** *bukkyō* **(shinto)-ni kyōmi-ga arimasu.**

Bible **baiburu, seisho**
Gospel **hukuinsho**
prayer **inori**
sermon **sekkyō**
service **reihai**
church **kyokai**
synagogue **yudaya-no kyōkai, shinagogu**
mission (building) **dendōkan**
mosque **mosku**
Buddhist temple **o-tera**
Shintoist shrine **jinja**

sect **shūha**

   Zen sect **Zen-shū**

monastery **sōin** (Buddhist); **shūdōin** (Christian)

bell tower **tō, shōrō**

priest **seishokusha**

   Father **shimpu**

   Orthodox **shisai**

   Buddhist **o-bō-san**

   Shinto **kannushi**

   rabbi **rabi**

monk **shūdōsō**

missionary **senkyōshi**

preacher **dendōshi**

oracle (written) **o-mikuji**

**Occupation (Shokugyō)**

At which company do you work? **Doko-ni o-tsutome desu ka?**

What is your profession? **Anata-no go-shokugyō-wa?**

What is your speciality? **Go-semmon-wa nan desu ka?**

What is your position? **Anata-no yakushoku-wa?**

I work…

   …at a company. **Watakushi-wa *kaisha*-ni tsutomete imasu.**

   …in an office. **…jimusho…**

   …at a factory. **…kōjō…**

   …in a research lab. **…kenkyūjo…**

   …at a publishing house. **…shuppansha…**

   …at a bank. **…ginkō…**

I'm a secretary. **Watakushi-wa** *hisho* **desu.**

   …scientist. **…kagakusha…**

   …journalist. **…jānarisuto…**

   …teacher. **…kyōshi…**

   …medical doctor. **…isha, ishi…**

   …attorney. **…bengoshi, hōteidairinin…**

   …engineer. **…gishi…**

   …lawyer. **…bengoshi…**

   …linguist. **…gengo-gakusha…**

   …art historian. **…rekishi-gakusha…**

   …accountant. **…kaikeishi…**

   …student (high school and up). **…gakusei…**

   …worker. **…rōdōsha…**

I'm an economist. **Watakushi-no semmon-wa keizai desu.**

How long have you been working in this firm? **Sono kaisha-ni-wa nannen o-tsutome desu ka?**

What kind of work do you do there? **Kaisha-de-wa nani-wo tantō-shite imasu ka?**


job **tsutome, shigoto**

work place **kimmusaki**

to work **shigoto-wo suru, hataraku**

plant **kōjō, puranto**

factory **kōba, kōjō**

office **yakusho, jimusho**

firm **kaisha**

publishing house **shuppansha**

ministry **shō**

post office **yūbinkyoku**

bank **ginkō**

position **shokuseki**
profession **shokugyō**
actress **joyū**
actor **danyū**
biologist **seibutsu-gakusha**
driver **untenshu**
housewife **shuhu**
zoologist **dōbutsu-gakusha**
historian **rekishika**
movie director **eiga kantoku**
ranger **shinrin-kanshiin**
pilot **pairotto, sōjūshi**
literary scholar **bungei-gakusha**
mathematician **sū gakusha**
physician **ishi**
writer **sakka**
poet **shijin**
artist **geijutsu-ka**
painter **gaka**
salesperson **ten'in**
priest (catholic) **shimpu**
pastor (protestant) **bokushi**
sociologist **shakai-gakusha**
scholar **gakusha**
physicist **butsuri-gakusha**
economist **keizai-gakusha**

## 16. SOCIALIZING & SMALL TALK

In this chapter, we give some useful expressions for situations in bars, informal gatherings and hanging out. The style of speech and vocabulary here is used mostly by young people. For some Japanese persons over thirty, it might not seem very polite, but anyhow, it's authentic, living Japanese!

### Making Friends

Have I seen you here before? **Koko-de mae-ni atta-koto aru?**

Are you having a good time? **Tanoshin deru?**

Yeah. **Uun.**

Yeah, having fun. **Tanoshii-yo!**

Shall we drink together? **Issho-ni nomanai?**

May I sit down? **Suwatte mo ii?**

What are you drinking? **Nani nonden-no?**

What's your name? **Namae wa?**

What? **Nani/E?**

Where do you live? **Doko-ni sunderu-no?**

Over there. (*answer if you don't want to be specific*) **Atchi.**

How old are you? **Toshi ikutsu?**

How old do I look? (*a common response*): **Ikutsu-ni mieru?**

What's your job? **Shigoto nani shiten-no?**

Are you a student? **Gakusei?**

What music do you like? **Donna ongaku-ga suki?**

Shall we dance? **Odoranai?**

I don't feel like dancing. **Mada odoranai.**

You are a good dancer. **Odori umai ne.**

How are you? **Genki?**

I'm fine. **Genki.**

All right. **Ii-yo.**

This is boring. *(m.)* **Tsumanne!** *(f.)* **Tsumannai!**

Let's get drunk! **Yopparaō!**

Good idea. **Ii kangae.**

Drink some more! **Motto nomeba!**

Are you drunk? **Yotteru?**

Maybe you'd better stop drinking. **Mō nomu-no yametara.**

Are you O.K.? **Daijōbu?**

You're nice. **Yasashii ne.**

Shall we leave? **Denai?**

Shall we go somewhere else? **Dokka ikanai?**

How does this sound? **Sore-de ii?**


I like it. **Suki.**

I hate it. **Kirai.**

I enjoy it. **Ureshii.**

I'm sad. **Kanashii.**

I want it (this thing). **Kore-ga hoshii.**

I don't want it. **Iranai** *(for things)*; **Ii** *(for things and actions)*.

I'm tired of it. **Mo akita.**

I'm confused. **Nandaka yoku wakaranai.**

I'm fine. **Daijōbu** *(when asked if you are all right)*.

I'm mad! **Atama-ni-kita!**

I'm tired. **Tsukareta.**

I'm surprised! **Odoroita!**

I'm sleepy. **Nemui.**

I'm scared. **Kowai.**

I feel sick. **Kimochi warui.**

I'm disappointed. **Gakkari shita-yo.**

I'm worried. *(m.)* **Shimpai-da.**

I made a mistake. **Machigatta.**

**Leaving**

I'll take you home. **Okutte iku yo.**

Do you want to drink morning coffee together?
**Yoake-no kōhi-wo issho-ni nomanai?** ("Let's spend the night together.")

I wanna know more about you. *(m.)* **Kimi-no koto motto shiritai.**

Shall we meet again? **Mata aeru?**

When can I see you next time? **Kondo itsu aeru?**

May I have your phone number? **Denwa bangō oshiete kureru?**

Take care. **Ki-wo tsukete ne.**

See you later. **Ja mata ne.**

I want to see you soon. **Sugu-ni aitai.**

Cool! **Kakkoii!**

Awesome/terrific. **Sugoi.**

Cute. **Kawaii.**

Chic. **Shibui.**

(You are) smart. **Atama-ga ii ne.**

Weird. **Kimochi warui.**

What a pity! **Kawaisō!**

Very bad. **Hidoi ne.**

Go for it! **Gambatte!**

Cheer up! *(m.)* **Genki dase yo!** *(f.)* **Genki dashite!**

Never mind. **Ki-ni shinai-de.**

idle chat **mandan**
hang out/ramble/stroll **sanpo, sozoro aruki**
bar **bā**
nightclub **naito kurabu**
discotheque **disuko**
rave (n.) **wameki, donari**
get drunk **you**
hangover **hutsuka yoi**
drunkenness **deisui**

**When it's not going well**

What's wrong? **Nanka atta-no?**
Nothing. **Betsu-ni.**
Leave me alone! **Hitori-ni shite!**
I'm not interested. *(m.)* **Kyomi nai-yo.**
Being with you is no fun. **Issho-ni ite mo
    tanoshikunai.**
You're boring. **Anata tsumannai.**
Don't bother me! *(f.)* **Jama shinai-de yo!**
Take your hands off! *(f.)* **Te-wo dokete yo!**
Please understand my feelings. *(m.)* **Boku-no
    kimochi wakatte.**
I'm happy to have known you. **Shiriatte yokatta.**
Forget it! **Yameta!**

**Meeting Again**

Do you have time? **Jikan aru?**
When is it good for you? **Itsu-ga ii?**
Then when? **Itsu-nara ii?**
About when? **Itsu goro?**
When can I come over? **Nanji-ni ikeba ii?**
Are you ready? **Mada?**
Soon. **Mō sugu.**

Maybe later. **Tabun kondo.** ("Maybe yes");
  **Sonouchi-ni ne.** ("Maybe no")
Someday. **Itsuka.** ("Maybe no")
Not now. **Ima ja nai.**
Always. **Itsumo.**
Not that day. **Sono hi dame.**

### Say/Listen/Look

Listen to me. **Kiite-yo.**
Do you hear me? **Kikoeta?**
I don't want to hear. **Kikitakunai.**
You'd better not say things like these. **Sonna koto itcha dame.**
Let's talk in English. **Eigo de hanasō.**
(I) understand. **Wakatta.**
I don't understand very well. **Yoku wakaranai.**
Talk about it later. **Sore-wa ato-de hanasō.**
Give me time to think about it. **Kangae-sasete.**
I don't want to talk. **Hanashitakunai.**
Speak more slowly. **Motto yukkuri itte.**
Say it again. **Mō ichido itte.**

Look at that! **Are mite!**
Don't look! *(m.)* **Miruna-yo!**
Did you see? **Mita?**
I didn't see. **Minakatta.**
I'll show you. **Misete ageru.**

### Come and Go

Come over. *(m.)* **Oide-yo.** *(f.)* **Kite.**
Can you come? **Koreru?**

# SOCIALIZING & SMALL TALK

Would you come with me? **Issho-ni konai?**
Where are you going? **Doko-ni iku-no?**
I can go/come. **Ikeru.**
I can't go. **Ikenai.**
I'm busy. **Isogashii.**
I'm coming. **Ima iku.**
I went/came. **Itta.**
I didn't go. **Ikanakatta.**
Don't go. **Ikanai-de.**
May I go? **Itte mo ii?**
Let's go. **Ikoo.**
I'm leaving soon. **Mō sugu deru.**

**Dating (Deto)**

For some adventurous visitors, knowing the right words in Japanese in the intimate situation might be very helpful.

You look beautiful. (*boy to girl*) **Kirei dayo.**
You have beautiful eyes. **Kirei-na hitomi da ne.**
I love you. **Aishiteru.**
I'm crazy about you. **Kimi-ni muchyū nanda.**
You're handsome. (*girl to boy*) **Suteki yo.**
You're sexy. (*boy to girl*) **Iroppoi!**
May I kiss you? **Kisu shite-mo ii?**
Kiss me. **Kisu shite.**
You have a beautiful body. (*boy to girl*) **Kirei-na karada da ne.**
Do you use contraceptives? (*boy to girl*) **Hinin shiteru?**
the Pill **hinin-yaku**
any contraceptive device **hinin-gu**

## 17. LEISURE

Detailed information on cultural events and enter-
taiment in Tokyo can be found in English-language
newpapers and in special magazines for foreigners
like *Tokyo Journal*, *Tokyo Weekender,* and *Tour
Companion* (these last two are published weekly
and distributed for free). *Tokyo Journal* contains a
lot of insider information for young and not so
young adventurers.

### Theater (Engeki)

Which theaters are the **most popular** in Tokyo?
**Tōkyo-de-wa donna gekidan-ga *yūmei* desu
ka?**

I'd like to see the No performance. **Nogaku-wo
mitai no desu ga.**

We'd like to go to the Kabuki theater.
**Watakushitachi-wa kabukiza-e itte mitai no
desu ga.**

I'd like to see a play of a **young** Japanese
**dramatist. Watakushi-wa nihon-no *wakai
gekisakka*-no shibai-wo mitai no desu.**

We'd like to see a Japanese ballet (**folk dance**).
**Watakushitachi-wa *nihon buyō* wo mitai no
desu.**

When was this theater founded? **Kono gekidan-wa
itsu goro dekita no desu ka?**

What is on stage here today? **Kyō-wa nani-wo
yatte imasu ka?**

Who **wrote** this play? **Kono gikyoku-wo *kaita*
no-wa dare desu ka?**

Who directed this performance? **Kono kōen-no enshutsusha-wa dare desu ka?**

This play was directed very well. **Kono shibai-wa yoku dekite imasu.**

How long is the performance? **Kōen-wa nan _jikan_ desu ka?**

How many acts has this play? **Kono gikyoku-wa _nan makumono_ desu ka?**

Who plays the **main character**? _Shuyaku_-wo enjiru nowa dare desu ka?

What does the main character's makeup **mean**? **Shuyaku-no meikyappu-ni-wa _donna imi_-ga arimasu ka?**

The acting of this actress (actor) is splendid. **Kono joyū (danyū-no engi-wa subarashii desu.**

This actress is very talented. **Kono joyū-wa saino-ga ārimasu ne.**

I enjoyed the performance very much. **Kono shibai-wa taihen ki-ni irimashita.**

actor **danyū**
actress **joyū**
intermission **makuai, kyūkei**
drama (art) **engeki**
theater (building) **gekijō**
theater (troupe) **gekidan**
stage **butai**
scene (part of performance) **bamen, maku**
repertoire **repātorii**
rehearsal **rihāsaru**
performance **kōen**
play **geki**
comedy **kigeki**

# LEISURE

tragedy **higeki**
playwright **geki-sakka**
producer **seisaku-sha**
stage manager **(butai) kantoku**

## Concert (Ongakukai)

Do you like **music**? *Ongaku*-ga suki desu ka?
I enjoy music very much. **Watakushi-wa ongaku-ga daisuki desu.**
Who is your favorite **composer**? **Anata-no o-suki-na** *sakkyokuka*-**wa dare desu ka?**
Where can I listen to a good **classical concert**? *Kurassikku* **no ii konsāto-wa doko de kikeru no desu ka?**
…concert of Japanese music? **Hōgaku…**
I'd like to listen to Japanese national instruments. **Watakushi-wa nihon no minzoku gakki-no konsāto-e ikitai no desu.**
I wish to attend a concert of the Tokyo Symphony Orchestra. **(Watakushi-wa) Tōkyō kōkyō gakudan-no konsāto-ni ikitai no desu.**
What is today's program? **Kyō no puroguramu wa nandesu ka?**
Who participates in the concert? **Konsāto-de-wa darega ensō suruno desu ka?**
Who is the conductor? **Kyō-no shikisha-wa dare desu ka?**
What's the name of this instrument? **Kono gakki-wa nanto iimasu ka?**
How did you like this concert? **Konsāto-wa ikaga deshita ka?**
I was very impressed. **Kandō shimashita.**

composer **sakkyokuka**
conductor **shikisha**
guitar **gitā**
instrument **gakki**
jazz **jazu**
music **ongaku**
orchestra **gakudan, ōkesutora**
organ **orugan**
piano **piano**
rock-n-roll **rokku-n-rōru**
song **uta**
symphony **simfonii, kōkyōkyoku**
symphony orchestra **kōkyō-gakudan, ōkesutora**
violin **baiorin**
vocal music **seigaku**
to play piano **piano-wo hiku**
to sing **utau**

### Cinema (Eiga)

I'd like to go to a cinema tonight. **Komban eiga-e/
-ni ikitai no desu ga.**

I'd like to see new Japanese movies. **(Watakushi-wa)
nihon-no atarashii eiga-wo mitai no desu.**

When was this film released? **Kono eiga-wa itsu
hūgiri-sareta no desu ka?**

Who is the director of this film? **Kono eiga-no
kantoku-wa dare desu ka?**

Who plays the principal character? **Shuyaku-wa
dare desu ka?**

In what movie theater can I see this film? **Sono
eiga-wa dono eigakan-de /joei-shite imasu
ka/mirare masu ka?**

How long is the screen time? **Jōei-jikan-wa donogurai desu ka?**

How do you like this film? **Eiga-wa ikaga deshita ka?**

This is a **good** (boring) film. **Kore wa *ii* (taikutsu) eiga desu.**

How much is a ticket? **Kippu-wa ikura desu ka?**

movie theater **eigakan**
movie/film **eiga**
suspense **sasupensu eiga**
detective movie **tantei eiga**
comedy **kigeki eiga**
action/adventures **akushon/bōken eiga**
producer **seisakusha**
director **kantoku**
screenplay writer **shinario-raitā**
camera-man **kameramen**
seat **seki**
balcony **nikaiseki**
ticket **kippu**
ticket window **kippu uriba**

**Museums and Exhibitions (Hakubutsukan to Tenrankai)**

I'd like to visit a **museum of Japanese art**. **(Watakushi-wa)** *nihon bijutsukan*-**e ikitai no desu.**

When was this museum founded? **Kono hakubutsukan-wa itsu dekita no desu ka?**

How much is the admission? **Nyūjōken-wa ikura desu ka?**

How long might it take to walk through the exhibition? **Tenji wo mite mawaru noni donokurai kakari masu ka?**

What can you recommend? **Nani ga osusume desu ka?**

Tell me please what I should not miss in this hall/pavillion? **Kono kan-de hikken no mono wo oshiete kudasai.**

We are interested in… **…-ni kyomi-ga arimasu.**

   …Japanese painting. **Nihon-no kaiga…**

   …contemporary Japanese art. **Nihon-no gendai bijutsu…**

   …traditional woodblock prints. **Dentōteki-na hanga…**

Where can I see works of Sesshū (Hokusai)?
   **Sesshū (Hokusai)-no sakuhin-wa dokode mirare masu ka?**
   **bijutsukan-ni aru no desu ka?**

In what hall are **ancient paintings** on display?
   *Kodai kaiga*-**wa dono hōru-ni /tenji sarete imasu ka/arimasu ka?**

What art exhibitions are open now? **Ima donna bijutsu tenrankai-ga hirakarete imasu ka?**

Can I take photos? **Koko-de shashin-wo totte mo iidesu ka?**

I cannot understand this picture (sculpture). **Kono e (chōkoku)-wa wakarimasen desu**.

To **what school** does this artist belong? **Kono gaka-wa *donna ryūha*-ni zoku-shite imasu ka?**

Most of all I like… **Ichiban ki-ni itta no-wa…desu.**

I saw many interesting and pleasant things.
   **Omoshirokute tanoshii sakuhin wo takusan mimashita.**

I enjoyed it. **Totemo yokatta desu.**
Where is the exit? **Deguchi-wa doko desu ka?**

exhibition **tenrankai**
museum **hakubutsukan**
painting exhibition **kaigaten**
book exhibition **shosekiten**
photography exhibit **shashinten**
press center **puresu-sentā**
pavilion **tenjikan**
visitor **kankyaku**
entrance **iriguchi**
entrance fee **nyūjōryō**
exit **deguchi**
viewing **kanran**
guidebook **annaisho, gaido bukku**

**Books (Dokusho)**

Do you like to read? (**Anata-wa**) **dokusho-ga
o-suki desu ka?**
Do you like literature? (**Anata-wa**) **bungaku-ga
o-suki desu ka?**
Do you have a large library? (**Anata-wa?**)
**zosho-wo takusan omochi desu ka?**
I'm interested in Japanese literature. (**Watakushi-
wa**) **nihon bungaku-ni kyōmi-ga arimasu.**
Have you read this book? **Kono hon-wo
yomimashita ka?**
No, I haven't. **Iie, yonde imasen.**
I recommend this novel. **Kono shōsetsu-wo
o-susume-shimasu.**

Do you read this story in the **original** language or in translation? **Kono monogatari-wa *gensho-de* soretomo honyaku de yonda no desu ka**?

Who is the author of this book? **Kono hon-no chosha-wa dare desu ka**?

May I borrow this book from you? **Kono hon-wo /kashite kudasaimasen ka/okari shitemo iidesuka?**

Give me something to read, please. **Nani ka yomu mono-wo kashite kudasai.**

Who is your **favorite writer** (poet)? **Anata-no *o-sukina sakka* (shijin)-wa dare desu ka?**

Who is the most popular writer in your country now? **O-kuni-de ima ichiban ninki-no aru sakka-wa dare desu ka?**

Have you read this author? **Kono sakka-no sakuhin-wo o-yomi-ni narimashita ka?**

I like the style of this author. **(Watakushi-wa) kono sakka-no buntai-ga suki desu.**

Summarize this story, please. **Kono monogatari-no *naiyō*-wo yōyakushite kudasai.**

How do you like this novel? **Kono shōsetsu-wa /ikaga/dō deshita ka?**

I didn't like it. It's boring. **Kono shōsetsu-wa yoku nakatta desu/Watashi wa sukidewa arimasen. Taikutsu desu.**

---

**Young People's Language**

*Have you read this book?* **Kono hon yonda?**
*Have you read this author?* **Kono sakka yonda?**
*I didn't like it. It's boring.* **Sukijanaine. Tsumannai.**

---

I'd like to **register** at the library. *Etsuran-tetsuzuki*-wo shitai no desu ga.

I'd like to obtain a **pass** to the main reading room (research reading room). **Ippan'yō (kenkyū'yō) etsuranshitsu-no** *etsuranken*-wo tsukutte itadakitai no desu ga.

Where is a catalog? **Hon-no katarogu-wa doko-ni arimasu ka?**

How do I fill in an **order slip**? **Hon-no** *seikyūhyō*-ni-wa dō kaitara ii no desu ka?

Give me *The Japan Times* newspaper for … year. **…nendo-no Japan Taimusu basami-wo kudasai.**

literature **bungaku, shoseki**
    classic literature **koten bungaku**
    children's literature **jidō bungaku**
    political literature **seiji shoseki**
    Japanese literature **nihon bungaku**
    contemporary literature **gendai bungaku**
author **chosha**
poet **shijin**
writer **sakka**
dramatist **gekisakka**
literary piece **sakuhin**
    drama **dorama**
    yearbook **nenkan**
    memoirs **kaisōroku**
    translation **honyakusho**
    original **gensho**
    story **monogatari**
    novel **shosetsu**
    classical Japanese novel **koten shōsetsu**

prose **sambun**

poem **tanka, haiku, shi**

classical Japanese poem **tanka, haiku, waka**

    poem of 31 syllables **tanka, waka**

    poem of 17 syllables **haiku**

    poem of linked verse **renga**

proverb **kotowaza**

play **gikyoku**

dictionary **jiten, jisho**

English-Japanese dictionary **Eiwa jiten (jisho)**

fairy tale **otogi-banashi**

complete works **sakuhinshū**

encyclopedia **hyakka-jiten**

humor **yūmoa sakuhin**

hero **hiiro, eiyū**

style **bunshō-no sutairu, buntai**

plot **purotto, suji**

image **keishō, imeiji**

book **hon**

    chapter **shō**

    title **hyōdai**

    cover **hyōshi**

    contents **mokuji**

    foreword **jobun**

    page **pēji**

    line **gyō**

publishing house **shuppansha**

bookstore **hon'ya, shoten**

library (public) **toshokan**

library (private) **zōsho**

to register at a library **etsuran-tetsuzuki-suru**

library card **etsuran-kādo**

reading room **etsuran-shitsu**

order slip **seikyūhyō**

## 18. SPORTS

What kind of sports/athletics are you into?
**Anata-wa donna supōtsu-wo shimasu ka?**

I do not work out a lot. **Watakushi-wa undō wa
amari shimasen.**

I like sports. **(Watakushi-wa) supōtsu daisuki
desu.**

I like athletics. **(Watakushi-wa) undō ga sukidesu.**

I **play** soccer, (basketball, tennis). **Watakushi-wa
sakkā (basukettobōru, tenisu)-wo *yatte*
imasu.**

I like skiing (skating, windsurfing). **(Watakushi-
wa) sukii (sukēto, windo sāfin) -wo yarimasu.**

I go rock climbing. **(Watakushi-wa) iwanobori
wo yatte imasu.**

I play chess. **(Watakushi-wa) chesu-wo yarimasu.**

I offer a draw (tie). **Hikiwake-ni shimashō.**

What kinds of sports are **popular** in your country?
**O-kuni-de wa donna supōtsu-ni *ninki*-ga
arimasu ka?**

I'd like to see gymnastics (boxing, sumo).
**Watakushi-wa taisō (bokusingu, sumō)-wo
mitai (no) desu.**

Who is the sumo champion of Japan? **Yokozuna-
wa dare desu ka?**

When does the game begin? **Shiai-wa itsu kara
hajimaru no desu ka/hajimari masu ka?**

How many rounds are in this match? **Kono shiai
wa nan raundo desu ka?**

This team plays very good. **Kono chiimu-wa
yūshū desu.**

This team plays pretty bad. **Kono chiimu-wa
tsuyoku nai desu (yowai desu).**

Who is the first? **Dare-ga ichii deshita ka?**

What's the score? **Sukoa-wa dō desu ka?**

What's the name of this player? **Ano senshu-wa nan toyū namae desu ka?**

Which baseball team is the best in Japan? **Nihon no yakyū-de wa doko-no chiimu-ga ichiban tsuyoi desu ka?**

What is his time? **Kare-no taimu-wa donogurai desu ka?**

He won. **Kare-wa kachimashita.**

athletics **undō**
sports **supōtsu**
rock climbing **iwanobori**
baseball **yakyū**
basketball **basukettobōru**
running/jogging **joggingu**
marathon **marason**
boxing **bokusingu**
wrestling **resuringu**
judo **jūdō**
karate **karate**
classic wrestling **gureko-roman-sutairu resuringu**
sumo **sumō**
bicycle riding **jitensha ni noru**
water sports **suijō kyōgi**
gymnastics **taisō**
mountain skiing **sangaku sukii**
horseback riding **bajutsu**
skating **sukēto**
sailing **seiringu**
swimming **suiei**
football (soccer) **sakkā**

team **chiimu**

captain **kyapten**

trainer **torēnā**

referee **referii, shinpan**

sportsman **senshu**

fan **fan**

match **shiai**

Olympic games **orimpikku taikai**

championship **senshuken-taikai**

start **sutāto**

finish **kesshōten**

record **kiroku**

to set a record **kiroku-wo yaburu**

to be the first **yūshō-suru**

chess **chesu**

## 19. EDUCATION

What is your educational history? **Anata-no gakureki-wa?**

I'm a college graduate. **Watakushi-wa daigaku sotsugyō desu.**

I study at a university now. **Watakushi-wa daigaku zaigaku desu.**

Where do you study? **Doko-de benkyō shite imasu ka.**

What's your most **difficult** course? **Anata-no ichiban *nigatena* kamoku-wa nan desu ka?**

When does the first (second) semester begin? **Ichi gakki-wa itsukara hajimarimasu ka?**

When does the summer vacation begin? **Natsuyasumi-wa itsukara desu ka?**

---

**Young People's Language**

*I failed an exam.* **Shiken-ni ochi te shi matta.**

*I passed an exam. (m.)* **Boku shiken-ni pasu-shita yo.**

*This year I'll have university entrance exams.* **Kotoshi boku wa daigaku-no nyugaku-shiken wo ukeru yo.**

*I'd like to go to medical school.* **Boku ika dai ni hairitai.**

---

academic degree **gakui**
advisor **shidō kyōkan**
auditorium/classroom **kyōshitsu**
college, university **daigaku**
 faculty of medicine **ika-daigaku, ika dai**

faculty of law **hōgaku-bu**
faculty of architecture **kenchiku-gakubu**
college graduate **gakushi**
course **kamoku**
    compulsory course **hisshū kamoku**
    free choice course **sentaku kamoku**
    difficult course **nigatena kamoku**
    course paper **gakunen-rombun**
    accounting **kaikei**
    algebra **daisu**
    biology **seibutsugaku**
    chemistry **kagaku**
    computer science **compyūta saiensu**
    geography **chirigaku**
    geometry **kikagaku**
    history **rekishi (gaku)**
    mathematics **sūgaku**
    medical science **igaku**
    programming **puroguramingu**
    physics **butsurigaku**
defense (of paper, dissertation) **rombun mensetsu**
department **kōza, gakubu**
doctor (Ph.D) **hakase**
education (academic record) **gakureki**
educational materials **kyōzai**
exam **shiken**
    to pass an exam **shiken-ni gōkaku suru**
    to fail **shiken-ni ochiru**
    to have the highest grade/100% **manten-wo toru**
faculty (division) **gakubu, ka**
graduation paper **sotsugyō rombun**
higher education **kōtō kyōiku**
homework **shukudai**

lecture (college level) **kōgi**
  to give a lecture **kōgi-wo suru**
lecture hall **kōdō**
lesson/lecture (general) **jugyō**
  to miss a lesson **jugyō-ni kesseki-suru**
  to do an assignment **shukudai-wo-suru**
research institute **kenkyūjo**
professor **kyōju**
semester **gakki**
seminar **zemināru, seminā**
to study/prepare (a subject) **manabu, benkyō suru,
  yoshū suru**
textbook **kyōkasho**
manual **setsumei-sho**
theme **tēma**

## 20. CONGRESS & CONFERENCE

When is the congress **open** (closed)? **Taikai-wa itsu** *kaikai* **(heikai) shimasu ka?**

When does **registration** start? **(Kaigi-no sankasha-no)** *tōroku***-wa itsu-kara desu ka?**

I'd like to know the program. **Nittei-wo oshiete kudasai.**

What is the procedure of sessions? **Kaigi-no puroguramu-wa dō natte imasu ka?**

Who is the session **chair** today? **Kyō-no** *gichō***-wa donata desu ka?**

When is the **next session**? **Kono** *tsugi-no kaigi***-wa itsu desu ka?**

I'll be speaking in English (French). **Watakushi-wa eigo (furansugo)-de hanasu tsumori desu.**

Will the translation be simultaneous or linear? **Tsūyaku-wa dōji-tsūyaku soretomo chikuji-tsūyaku desu ka?**

congress **taikai**
conference **kaigi**
program **nittei**
symposium **simpoziumu**
consultation **sōdankai**
presidium **gichōdan**
organizing committee **un'ei iinkai**
secretariat **jimukyoku**
guest(s) **raihin**
to participate **sanka-suru**
registration **tōroku**
cultural exchange **bunka-kōryū**
academic contacts **gakujutsu kōryū**

delegation **daihyōdan**
   youth delegation **seinen daihyōdan**
   sports delegation **supōtsu daihyōdan**
host (organization) **shotaigawa**
to speak (present a paper) **hatsugen-suru**
section sessions **bunkakai**
interpretation **tsūyaku**
   simultaneous interpretation **dōji tsūyaku**
   linear interpretation **chikuji tsūyaku**
press conference **kisha-kaiken**
press center **puresu-sentā**
printed materials **insatsu-shiryō**

## 21. WEATHER & CLIMATE

It's such wonderful weather today. **Kyōwa totemo ii o-tenki desu ne.**

Today is very **hot. Kyōwa totemo *atsui* desu.**

   … muggy.   **…mushiatsui…**

   … warm.   **…atatakai…**

   … cold.   **…samui…**

   … chilly.   **…usurasamui…**

Today is horrible weather. **Kyō-wa iyana tenki desu.**

Today is misty. **Kyo-wa kiri-ga kakatte imasu.**

There was a snowfall last night. **Sakuya yuki-ga furimashita.**

What's the temperature today? **Kyō-no kion-wa dono kurai desu ka?**

It's a very hot summer this year, isn't it? **Kotoshi-no natsu-wa taihen atsui desu ne.**

When do the cherries begin to blossom? **Sakura-wa itsugoro sakimasu ka?**

When does the rainy season begin? **Nyūbai-wa itsu goro desu ka?**

What is the forecast for today (tomorrow)? **Kyō no tenki yohō wa dō desu ka?**

Today (tomorrow) will be… **Kyo (ashita)-wa… tenki ni narudesho/hareru deshō/kumoru deshō/ame deshō.**

   …sunshine.   **…hareta…**

   …cloudy.   **… kumotta, kumori-no…**

   …rainy.   **…amemoyō-no…**

   …wet.   **…zime-zime-shita…**

It's getting better. **Tenki-ga yoku natte kimashita.**

It's getting worse. **Tenki-ga kuzurete kimashita.**

It looks as if it'll be raining soon. **Osoraku ame-ni naru deshō.**

Is it raining now? **Ima ame-ga futte imasu ka?**

What's the water temperature today? **Kyō-no suion-wa donogurai nando desu ka?**

The dawn (morning glow) here is so beautiful! **Kireina asayake desu ne!**

The dusk (evening glow) here is so beautiful! **Kireina yūyake desu ne!**

The sky begins to lighten. **Sora ga akaruku natte kimashita.**

The **sunrise** (sunset) is coming soon. *Hinode* (nichibotsu)-wa mō sugu desu.

Is the typhoon coming to Japan? **Taihū-wa Nihon-ni kimasu ka?**

Where is the epicenter of the earthquake? **Shingen-chi-wa doko desu ka?**

How much (on the scale) is a seismic disturbance? **Shindo-wa donogurai desu ka?**

Yesterday there was a volcano eruption. **Kinō kazan-ga hunka-shimashita.**

climate **kikō**
    mild climate **onwana kikō**
    harsh climate **kibishii kikō**
    sea climate **kaiyōsei kikō**
moon **tsuki**
star **hoshi**
sun **taiyō**
humidity **shitsudo**
season **kisetsu**
    spring **haru**

summer **natsu**
autumn **aki**
winter **huyu**
weather **tenki**
rainy weather **amemoyō-no tenki**
cloudy weather **kumotta tenki**
bad weather **warui tenki**
good weather **yoi/ii tenki**

air temperature **kion**
water temperature **suion**
cold **samui, tsumetai**
cool **suzushii**
chilly **usurasamui**
hot **atsui**
muggy **mushiatsui**
warm **atatakai**

air/atmosphere **taiki**
clear **hare**
cloud **kumo**
cloudy **kumori**
dew **tsuyu**
frost **shimo**
haze **kasumi**
ice **kōri**
mist/fog **kiri**
thick fog **nōmu**
rain cloud **amagumo**
rain **ame**
sleet **mizore**
snow **yuki**
melting **yukidoke**

wind **kaze**
the wind begins to blow **kaze-ga dete kimashita**

natural disaster **saigai, tensai**
volcano **kazan**
active volcano **katsu kazan**
volcano's eruption **kazan-no hunka**
earthquake **jishin**
epicenter **shingenchi**
flood **kōzui**
typhoon **taihū** (stronger); **bōhūu**
storm **arashi**
approaching (about a storm) **sekkin-suru**

## 22. NUMBERS & MEASURES

There are two sets of words designating numbers in Japanese language: original Japanese numbers and numbers borrowed from China. Japanese numbers (1 to 10) are used for concrete counting: **hitotsu-no heya** ("one room"), **futatsu-no isu** ("two chairs"). Chinese numbers are used for abstract counting. When used for counting things and objects, they are added with special counting suffixes.

### CARDINAL NUMBERS

**Japanese Numbers**

| | |
|---|---|
| 1 | **hitotsu** |
| 2 | **hutatsu** |
| 3 | **mittsu** |
| 4 | **yottsu** |
| 5 | **itsutsu** |
| 6 | **muttsu** |
| 7 | **nanatsu** |
| 8 | **yattsu** |
| 9 | **kokonotsu** |
| 10 | **tō** |

**Chinese Numbers**

| | |
|---|---|
| 0 | **rei** |
| 1 | **ichi** |
| 2 | **ni** |
| 3 | **san** |
| 4 | **shi** |

| | |
|---|---|
| 5 | **go** |
| 6 | **roku** |
| 7 | **shichi** or **nana** |
| 8 | **hachi** |
| 9 | **ku**, **kyū** |
| 10 | **jū** |
| 11 | **jū ichi** |
| 12 | **jū ni** |
| ... | |
| 20 | **nijū** |
| 21 | **nijū ichi** |
| 22 | **nijū ni** |
| ... | |
| 30 | **sanjū** |
| 31 | **sanjū ichi** |
| 32 | **sanjū ni** |
| ... | |
| 40 | **yonjū, shijū** |
| 50 | **gojū** |
| 60 | **rokujū** |
| 70 | **shichijū** or **nanajū** |
| 80 | **hachijū** |
| 90 | **kujū** or **kyūjū** |
| 100 | **hyaku** |
| 123 | **hyaku nijū san** |
| ... | |
| 200 | **nihyaku** |
| 300 | **sambyaku** |
| 400 | **yonhyaku** |
| 500 | **gohyaku** |
| 600 | **roppyaku** |
| 700 | **nanahyaku** |
| 800 | **happyaku** |
| 900 | **kyūhyaku** |

# NUMBERS & MEASURES

| | |
|---|---|
| 1000 | **sen** |
| 2000 | **nisen** |
| ... | |
| 10,000 | **ichiman** |
| 20,000 | **niman** |
| 30,000 | **sanman** |
| ... | |
| 100,000 | **jūman** |
| 1,000,000 | **hyakuman** |
| 100,000,000 | **ichioku** |

## ORDINAL NUMBERS

| | |
|---|---|
| first | **dai-ichi, ichiban no** |
| second | **dai-ni, niban no** |
| third | **dai-san, samban no** |
| fourth | **dai-yon-no** |
| fifth | **dai-go-no** |
| sixth | **dai-roku-no** |
| seventh | **dai-shichi-no** |
| eighth | **dai-hachi-no** |
| ninth | **dai-kyū-no** |
| tenth | **dai-jū-no** |
| eleventh | **dai-jū ichi-no** |
| | |
| half | **han** |
| one-half | **nibun-no ichi, hanbun** |
| one-quarter | **yonbun-no ichi, shihanbun** |
| one-third | **sambun-no ichi** |
| 2.5 | **ni ten go** |
| | |
| percent | **pāsento** |
| 1% | **ichi pāsento** |
| 25% | **nijū go pāsento** |

## MEASURES

| | |
|---|---|
| meter | **mētoru** |
| centimeter | **senchimētoru** |
| kilometer | **kiro, kiromētoru** |
| foot | **fiito** |
| mile | **mairu** |
| | |
| gram | **guramu** |
| kilogram | **kiroguramu** |
| pound | **pondo** |
| ounce | **onsu** |
| | |
| liter | **rittoru** |
| gallon | **garon** |

## 23. TIME

time **toki, jikan, jikoku**

morning **asa**
day (as opposed to night) **hiru, hiruma**
evening **ban, yūgata**
night **yoru**
midday, noon **shōgo**
midnight **(ma)yonaka**
before noon **gozen**
after noon **gogo**

Adding a suffix *-ni* to the above words means "in the morning," "in the evening," etc.

### Day

day (24 hours) **nichi**
one day **ichinichi**
two days **futsuka-kan**
three days **mikka-kan**
four days **yokka-kan**
five days **itsuka-kan**
six days **muika-kan**
seven days **nanuka-kan**
eight days **yōka-kan**
nine days **kokonoka-kan**
ten days **tōka-kan**
twenty days **hatsuka-kan**

today **kyō, konnichi** (nowadays)
yesterday **kinō**

tomorrow **ashita**
the day before yesterday **ototoi, issakujitsu**
the day after tomorrow **asatte, myogonichi**

## Hours and Minutes (Ji soshite Hun)

hour **ji**
minute **hun, pun**
second **byō**
What's the time? **Nan-ji desu ka?**
Six o'clock. **Roku-ji desu.**
Seven in the morning. **Gozen shichi-ji desu.**
Eight in the evening. **Gogo hachi-ji desu.**
It's 12:15 now. **Ima jūni-ji jūgo-hun desu.**
It's half past nine. **Hachi-ji-han desu.**
Five minutes to three. **Sanji gohun mae desu.**

## Days of the Week (Yōbi)

Monday **getsuyōbi** (Moon's day)
Tuesday **kayōbi** (Fire's day)
Wednesday **suiyōbi** (Water's day)
Thursday **mokuyōbi** (Tree's day)
Friday **kin'yōbi** (Gold's day)
Saturday **doyōbi** (Earth's day)
Sunday **nichiyōbi** (Sun's day)

What is the day of the week today? **Kyō-wa
    naniyōbi desu ka?**
this week **konshū**
last week **senshū**
next week **raishū**
one week **isshūkan**
two weeks **nishūkan**

**Months (Tsuki)**

January **ichigatsu**
February **nigatsu**
March **sangatsu**
April **shigatsu**
May **gogatsu**
June **rokugatsu**
July **shichigatsu**
August **hachigatsu**
September **kugatsu**
October **jūgatsu**
November **jūichigatsu**
December **jūnigatsu**

this month **kongetsu**
last month **sengetsu**
next month **raigetsu**
one month **ikkagetsukan**
two months **nikagetsukan**

**Years (Toshi)**

There are two calendar systems in Japan: Western and Japanese, based on the eras of imperial rule. The present era, the *Heisei* era, began in 1989 when the emperor Akahito was enthroned. It was the first year of the Heisei era (Heisei 1), so the year 2000 is Heisei 12.

this year **kotoshi**
last year **kyonen, sakunen**
next year **rainen**

one year **ichinenkan**
calendar (Emperor's) era **nengō**

year 1999 **sen kyūhyaku kyūjū kyū nen**
year 2001 **nisen ichi nen**
I was born in 1975. **Watakushi-wa sen kyūhyaku nanajū go nen umare desu.**

All these words are used after the noun:
before **mae-ni**
after **ato-de**
between, during **...-no aida-ni**

Before the movie I went to a bookstore. **Eiga-no mae-ni hon'ya-ni ikimashita.**
Let's go there after dinner. **Chūshoku/Ohirugohan-no ato-de soko-e ikimashō.**
Yesterday I spent five hours in the museum. **Kinō goji-kan-mo hakubutsukan-ni imashita.**

## 24. EMERGENCY

Help! **Tasukete kure!**

Could you help me, please. **Tetsudatte kudasai.**

Where is the nearest **telephone**? **Ichiban chikai** *denwa*-**wa doko desu ka?**

Call the police. (Send a **policeman**.) *Keikan*-**wo yonde kudasai**.

Call an **ambulance**. *Kyūkyūsha*-**wo yonde kudasai.**

Is there a **doctor** near here? **Kono chikaku-ni** *isha*-**wa imasu ka?**

Where is the **pharmacy**? *Kusuriya* **ma doko desu ka?**

Take me to a **hospital**. *Byōin*-**e tsurete itte kudasai.**

There's been an **accident**. *Jiko* **ga arimashita/ okorimashita.**

Go away! **Atchie ike!**

Get out of here! **Dete ike!**

I'm **lost**. (**Watakushi-wa**) *michi-ni mayotte* **shimaimashita/mayoi mashita.**

I am **ill**. (**Watakushi-wa**) *byōki* **desu.**

I've been **robbed**. (**Watakushi-wa**) *dorobō*-**ni aimashita.**

They **robbed** me. **Kakera ga watashikara ryakudatsu shimashita.**

I have lost my... **...-wo nakushimatta.**

...bag. **Kaban, fukuro...**

...camera. **Kamera...**

...laptop. **Rapputoppu kompyūtā...**

...money. **O-kane...**

...passport. **Pasupōto...**

...wallet. **Saihu...**

I apologize. **Gomen nasai! O-wabi-shimasu.**

Excuse me. **Shitsurei itashimasu.**

I am sorry. **Mōshiwake arimasen.**

I want to contact my **embassy. (Watakushi-wa)**
    *taishikan* **to renraku-wo toritai no desu ga.**

I need an interpreter. *Tsūyaku*-**wo o-negai-**
    **shimasu.**

---

**Young People's Language**

*Get away!* **Mukō e itte-yo!** *(girl speaking)*

*Go somewhere!* **Dokka ike-yo!** *(boy speaking)*

*What a nasty guy!* **Yanayatsu!** *(girl speaking)*

*Take your hands off!* **Te-wo dokete yo!** *(girl*
    *speaking);* **Dokero!** *(boy speaking)*

*Don't touch me!* **Sawannai-de!** *(girl speaking);*
    **Samaru-na!** *(boy speaking)*

*I think you're trying to trick me!* **Damasō-to**
    **shiteru-no**! *(girl speaking)*

*Don't think that I don't know anything!*
    **Damasarenai-zo!** *(boy speaking);*
    **Damasarenai wayo!** *(girl speaking)*

*Is this because I'm a foreigner (American)?*
    **Gaijin (Amerika-jin) da kara?**

*I want to see the manager!* **Manejā yonde**
    **kure-yo!** *(boy speaking);* **Manejā yonde**
    **kudasai!** *(both genders).*

---

## 25. JAPANESE SIGNS & INSCRIPTIONS

Information 案内所 (annaijo)
Information 受付 (uketsuke)

Open (shop) 開店 (kaiten)
Open 営業中 (eigyochu)
Closed (day off) 休業 (kyugyo)
Closed (shop) 閉店 (heiten)
Closed (under preparation—will open later) 準備中 (jumbichu)

Danger! Beware! 危険 (kiken)
Stop! 止まれ (tomare)
No entrance 立入禁止 (tachiiri kinshi)
Road closed 通行止め (tsuko dome)
No Smoking! 禁煙 (kin'en)

Entrance 入口 (iriguchi)
Exit 出口 (deguchi)
Push (the door) 押す (osu)
Pull (the door) 引く (hiku)

Gentlemen's room 男子用 (danshiyo)
Ladies' room 女子用 (joshiyo)
Toilet トイレ (toire)
Toilet お手洗い (o-tearai)